So you want to
publish a magazine?

Angharad Lewis

Laurence King Publishing

My respect and gratitude go to the many magazine makers and publishing industry professionals who have generously contributed their knowledge to this book. Thanks also to everyone at Laurence King, particularly Sara Goldsmith for her hard work, patience and resourceful editing. Lastly, thank you Reuben for your unstinting support.

Published in 2016 by
Laurence King Publishing Ltd
361–373 City Road
London EC1V 1LR
e-mail: enquiries@laurenceking.com
www.laurenceking.com

© Text 2016 Angharad Lewis

Commissioned images on pages 32, 46, 70, 84, 106, 136 and 146 © Ivan Jones

A catalogue record for this book is available from the British Library.

ISBN: 978-1-78067-754-5

Design by She Was Only

Printed in China

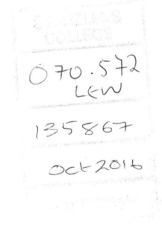

Preface
Angharad Lewis

This book is not intended to map a definitive path or conjure magic formulae for publishing a magazine. Its focus is the world of independent magazine publishing, where rules are being broken and models redefined more quickly than any book could seek to capture. I have instead attempted to bring together the knowledge and experience of the indie publishers already making wonderful, inventive magazines, and to represent the poles of indie publishing – from bedroom projects to successful business ventures – and the significant points in between. It is for the reader to find his or her own pathway through the publishing landscape, but I hope this book will be a trusty companion.

Foreword
Jeremy Leslie, Creative Director
at MagCulture

Over the last ten to fifteen years independent magazine makers have grasped new technologies – the very technologies that were supposed to kill print publishing – to prove that when produced with the right measure of care and attention, printed magazines still have plenty to offer our information-saturated world.

Against a background of over-commoditized mainstream publications and free online content, these independents have established new approaches to traditional subjects like sport, fashion and food, as well taking advantage of their position to question the very essence of what a magazine is.

They have rediscovered the sensual overload of print, combining touch, smell and sound with the visual to provide the perfect antidote to our flat, shiny digital habit.

TV, radio and newspapers have noted the rise of the indie magazine; barely a week goes by without another website offering an 'Our top ten indies' list, and mainstream publishers now regularly pay lip service to their existence. It's an international phenomenon, the Internet providing a global platform and events like Printout (London), Indiecon (Hamburg) and U-Symposium (Singapore) spreading the word and introducing the magazines and their makers to audiences keen to get involved themselves.

But what does it take to make an independent magazine? Can they be successful businesses in their own right? Can the form continue to develop and grow in popularity?

In this book, we hear from many of the most important voices in independent magazines as they offer insight into their working process, their ambitions for their projects and the ups and downs of self-publishing. It's an essential addition to the bookshelf of anyone interested in the business of magazine publishing as much as the creative side.

Introduction
Angharad Lewis

The aim of this book is to be a companion to independent magazine publishing. It is full of insider knowledge about every aspect of making and publishing a magazine, from drawing board to delivery and beyond. Whether you are already making a magazine, planning one or dreaming of doing it one day, you should find plenty here to inspire and aid you in your quest. We will peel back the layers of independent publishing to find out what creates the mystique and also to give a realistic view of making your own magazine and getting it into readers' hands.

This book represents the experience and insight of more than 50 people from the world of independent magazine publishing. Most are practising magazine-makers; others are experts in the wider world of publishing, from distribution to retail to printing. All were interviewed exclusively for this book. Each chapter includes case studies of magazines and their individual approaches to a particular theme or challenge. Between the chapters are longer interviews with key players from each step of the publishing process, revealing intimate professional views on how their businesses run, and offering invaluable advice to those starting out.

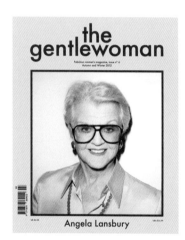

the
gentlewoman

Angela Lansbury

1.

There have been several times in the history of magazines when independent publishing has had 'a moment', but today it has taken on the momentum of a movement. There have never been so many people pursuing their own publishing ventures, despite – or perhaps because of – the failing state of large-scale commercial print publishing. Nimble-footed, small but perfectly formed magazines, with multitaskers at their helms capitalizing on the finer physical quality of print, have been able to carve out important niches in the voids left by mass-market media. Audiences are hungry for magazines made with integrity, by and about real people, and they want to consume these titles in new ways.

Do you read me?

Women in
Publishing in
the Middle
East and
North Africa

2.

3.

The
Gourmand

A food and culture journal

4.

The BOX
THAT
SHRANK
THE
WORLD

5.

1. *The Gentlewoman*, issue 6, Autumn/Winter 2012, Angela Lansbury, photographed by Terry Richardson

2. *Riposte*, issue 2, Summer 2014, article looking at publishing in the Middle East

3. *Mono.kultur*, issue 33, Spring 2013, Kim Gordon, featuring artworks by Gordon printed on various insert papers

4. *The Gourmand*, issue 4, 2014, cover, featuring photography by Thomas Pico for a special report on chocolate

5. *Works That Work*, issue 2, 2013, article examining how the lowly shipping container has helped transform world economics

6. *Delayed Gratification*, issue 12, 2014, article about an electrical ongineer from Derby, UK, who became a king in Nigeria

The last King of Derby

6.

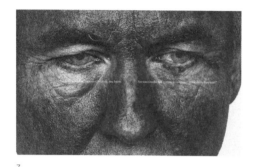

7.

8.

9.

7. *Port*, issue 15, Autumn 2014, spread from article about renowned composer Esa-Pekka Salonen, photographed by Pieter Hugo

8. *The Ride*, issue 8, 2014, front and back cover illustration by Shan Jiang. The cycling journal stands out among its rivals for its story-telling editorial and creative use of illustration and photography

9. *Wrap*, issue 10, Spring/Summer 2014. The magazine, which began showcasing illustrators' work in the form of bound sheets of wrapping paper, has evolved into a perfect-bound design and culture title

10. *Printed Pages*, issue 6, Summer 2014, article about David Pearson's book designs. *Printed Pages* is the second printed incarnation of the online platform It's Nice That and creative agency INT Works

11. *The White Review*, issue 9, December 2013. Probably the world's most beautiful art magazine, it is a joyful print experience, with bound cover, regular tipped- and bound-in reproductions and postcard inserts

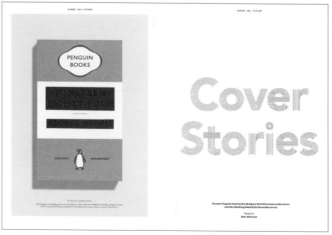

10.

The beauty of independence is the freedom to choose exactly how you will make and sell your magazine. You are not tied to the conventions and prescribed ways of doing things dictated by the corporate, mainstream publishing world. You can choose to set up your magazine and business in a way that suits your pocket and your way of working.

On the other hand, you will have to learn fast and do almost everything yourself; you will make a lot of mistakes along the way and, it is to be hoped, learn from them. Making mistakes can be positive, but this book will help you to avoid potentially disastrous pitfalls and arm you with know-how from the indie publishers who have gone before.

11.

In some ways it has never been easier to publish a magazine, but there are also unprecedented challenges to be faced. Much of the industry is still dominated by outmoded structures based on mass commercial publishing; distribution and advertising are two key problem areas for independents. But heartening innovations are being made by ingenious magazine-makers circumventing traditional approaches to publishing. While the independents do not have economies of scale on their side, they increasingly have strength in numbers as they form communities and share their knowledge and experience.

This book is born out of that community spirit, and has come about entirely through the generosity of all the publishers who have contributed to it. Regardless of the mountains that independent publishers have to climb, their reward comes from the ever-growing army of readers who are in love with magazines.

"Being the reader of a magazine is a badge … Print will always have this very intriguing, intimate appeal. It has a glamour that people want to be associated with."
— Cathy Olmedillas, publisher and editor, *Anorak*

01

So you want to publish a magazine?

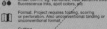

Medium / Stock
Special paper or material
or use multiple paper stock

Ink. Printed with inks other than conventional
offset CMYK, eg: varnishes, heat sensitive inks,
fluorescence inks, spot colors, etc

Format. Project requires folding, scoring
or perforation. Also unconventional binding or
unconventional format.

Cutting
Lazer cutting,
Die cutting, etc

Gold Foiling
Embossing
Letterpressing Stamping

Add on materials.
Hand crafted project

First things first: essential questions to ask yourself

There is no denying the irresistible qualities of magazines: they capture our imagination, make us feel part of something and link us to new ideas. Their frequency as publications acts as a metronome of the new in our lives: we eagerly await each issue, devour it and then begin anticipating the next fix. But beyond the magic of the design and content is a different reality – a mad, bad and sometimes humdrum back room, where people toil for inconceivably long hours.

In our dreams, the magazine we love is created in a fantastical space. The reality is often a messy office at the top of too many flights of stairs in a cheap part of town, or a space cleared on someone's kitchen table. For the many independent publishers of the world, however, that is not a turn-off, but rather part of the buzz. Out of all that chaos and sweat comes something beautiful that will sit proudly on the bookshop shelf or make its way through hundreds or thousands of letterboxes around the world. This chapter is 'return to Go': a look at how you can set out your stall as a magazine – to define clearly what you want your magazine to be and what you want to achieve by publishing it. You will probably change your mind a hundred times along the way, and keep making mistakes, but the beauty of magazines is that there is always another issue in which you can fix what's not working and try something new.

In this book, independent publishers reveal the important questions you should ask as you set out on your adventure in independent publishing. There are no right or wrong answers, because there are as many reasons for and ways to go about making a magazine as there are publishers, but thinking about these conundrums and challenges should be the backbone of your enterprise.

1.

"Ask yourself, what are you in it for?"

Kai von Rabenau, *Mono.kultur*

Very few independent magazines are just a magazine, and of those that are, fewer still are run as stand-alone businesses or full-time, paid occupations for the makers. For most people who publish a magazine, that is just one part of what they do; they might also have a day job to pay the bills, or run a related business such as a shop or design studio. Nevertheless, taking on the massive workload of a magazine is driven by a need or a passion; it could be an individual's obsession with a subject or hobby, such as poetry or cycling, or the magazine might be part of a bigger business model, providing a showcase for a particular product or service and attracting new clients.

1. *Mono.kultur*, issue 32, Summer 2012, Martino Gamper

2. *Lucky Peach*, issue 10, February 2014

3. *PIN-UP*, issue 16, Spring/Summer 2014

4. *Cereal*, issue 5, 2014

Monocle magazine is often cited as a pioneering example of a successful independent publishing model. In September 2014 it was valued at $15 million after it sold a 5 per cent share to the publishing arm of the Japanese news agency Nikkei.

The magazine is just part of a brand that also includes a shop, a radio station and cafes, all run in parallel with editor-in-chief Tyler Brûlé's successful high-end branding agency, Winkreative.

Read an interview with Tyler Brûlé on pages 122–27

This type of multifaceted model can apply on many different scales. At the opposite end of the spectrum from *Monocle*, but no less important to the thousand or so people who buy each issue, *The Shelf Journal* is a playground and showcase for the creativity of the graphic designers Morgane Rébulard and Colin Caradec, who produce it in Paris. Their magazine pays homage to editorial design and 'the cult of the shelf'.

So ask yourself what your goals are. How ambitious are you? Is your magazine going to be your main occupation – a profitable venture – or a part-time creative outlet?

"What is the function of print today, and can I create value in this medium?"

Adam Krefman, *Lucky Peach*

2.

It has never been easier to make and publish a magazine. Desktop technology puts design and print production at the fingertips of anyone who is willing to learn the basics; commercial printers in a squeezed market are increasingly happy to take on small-run jobs to reach new customers; and independent shops enthusiastically take on small titles to create a unique offering for shoppers and justify their existence in competition with high-street chains and online retailers.

But this is also an extremely competitive world. If you're trying to attract readers in bookshops and newsagents, yours will be one of many new titles every month, up against established favourites. Sasha Simic of the independent UK distributor Central Books reports that he is approached every week by three or four new magazines seeking distribution.

Read an interview with distributor Sasha Simic on pages 84–87

This competition ensures high standards of design and editorial, since magazines rise and fall on the merits of their offering to the reader, and quality is essential to that. 'The idea that print is dead comes up again and again,' says Matt Willey, creative director of *Port* and the *New York Times Magazine*. 'Print isn't dead. And right now is a really, really interesting moment. But you have to justify your presence in print, which is a good thing.'

"What is so special and unique about my idea that I'm killing trees for it?"

Felix Burrichter, *PIN-UP*

3.

A printed magazine has an archival quality; it can be there on your shelf for many years. A good magazine honours that privilege, and the trees that were felled to make it, by producing content that lives up to being looked at again and again for years to come.

Today, anyone publishing in print has a duty to think responsibly about the resources they are using. Many independent publishers take pride in choosing recycled or FSC-certified paper stocks and environmentally friendly non-toxic inks. This is something you should include in conversations with your printer when you are asking for quotations and specifying your print job (see page 142).

Be sure that what you're publishing justifies the time, effort and expense of a print format, since there is no point serving something up in a magazine that is better suited to a blog or website. The appetite of print consumers is tending towards unique, beautiful content that deserves to be treasured.

As David Lane, editor in chief and creative director of *The Gourmand*, says, 'people love good-quality content and production. Books look nicer on bookshelves than hard drives.' The sentiment is echoed by Andrew Diprose, who by day is the art director of Condé Nast's UK edition of *Wired*, and by night makes the indie cycling magazine *The Ride Journal*: 'If you're not trying to put out something of quality and you don't have integrity, then I don't think it's worth doing.'

"Print and digital are equally important for the business."

Rosa Park, *Cereal*

See *Printed Pages* case study on page 82

4.

If you're a printed magazine, having an online presence is essential. At the very least, it's a quick reference point for readers, and it could also be an important partner to the magazine in terms of content. The web can perform tricks that are alien to print, such as allowing you to publish news in a matter of minutes, host film and animation, and make intelligent connections using the power of the click.

There are many examples of magazines that began life as blogs before becoming printed objects. Publishing online can build a loyal readership, some of whom can be translated into customers of a printed publication. Will Hudson of *It's Nice That* explains that when he and his partner, Alex Bec, launched their first eponymous magazine title, in 2009 (since superseded by *Printed Pages*), it was to an eager audience, ripe for conversion into print readers. A magazine is nothing without its readers.

"Do I have a unique idea? Is there an audience for it?"

David Lane, *The Gourmand*

5.

You may care passionately about your subject, but you must make something that other people will regard with equal fervour. And that's just the tip of the iceberg. Once you've established that there is an audience for your magazine, you must let enough people know about it, inspire them to buy it, and keep delivering content and design that make them crave the next instalment.

'Niche' needn't mean 'irrelevant', especially if your idea genuinely taps an uncared-for market. Andrew and Philip Diprose's *The Ride Journal* prints a modest 5,000–6,000 copies of each issue, but they sell out to an eager audience of bicycle enthusiasts who appreciate the unique blend of story-telling, illustration and photography. The title has identified a market of cyclists who are interested in the experience of cycling, rather than the kit and caboodle touted in most other bike magazines.

See *The Ride Journal* case study on page 26

"Are you bringing something new to your project?"

Elana Schlenker, *Gratuitous Type*

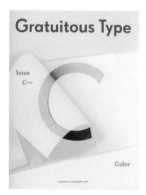

6.

The world of independent publishing is tough enough without trying to publish a magazine that already exists. Your idea and your voice must be original. As Cathy Olmedillas, founder and publisher of the pioneering kids' magazine *Anorak*, points out, 'if you're selling 20,000 copies of any independent mag you're doing flipping well. If you have one magazine doing that, fantastic – but if you have 20, they can't possibly all survive.'

Hudson agrees: 'Have a point of difference,' he says. 'Have a reason to exist. Don't just ape someone's style and content – if that's what you're desperately passionate about, then get in touch with those people, go and work for them, go and make that thing better.'

'The independent publishing world is full of incredible publications that are unique and inspiring and just make my jaw drop,' says Elana Schlenker of typography magazine *Gratuitous Type*. 'It's also full of copycats … who pick up a copy of *Apartamento* or *The Gentlewoman* – both amazing – and just try to make the same thing.'

"Do I really want this? Indie publishing isn't a career or a decent-paying job. It's a lifestyle."

Chris Ng, *IdN*

7.

However you approach making a magazine, you need to be seriously dedicated. As everyone in independent publishing will tell you, it's extremely hard work and will take over your life; when the fun jobs of putting together the editorial and design are over, you'll be up until the small hours ordering bar codes, collating orders for your fulfilment house, responding to readers' cries of 'Where's my copy?' and working out the print schedule for the next issue.

Jefferson Hack, founder of *Dazed & Confused*, *AnOther* and *AnOther Man*, lives and breathes the world of his titles. 'If you're going to do it,' he says, 'you've really got to live it. Even if it's not something you can do full-time, it has to be your primary passion. I think a good magazine is a great obsession. And a really great magazine is a great obsession taken even further.'

Read an interview with Jefferson Hack on pages 16–19

"Are you prepared for all the unglamorous jobs – marketing, distribution, finances, taxes, stuffing hundreds of envelopes?"

Rob Orchard, *Delayed Gratification*

8.

Jeremy Leslie, the founder of MagCulture and author of *The Modern Magazine: Visual Journalism in the Digital Era* (2013), says that if anyone approaches him for advice about how to make a magazine, his first response is 'Don't do it.' If, at that, your resolve falters for so much as a microsecond, you might as well throw in the towel now, he says, only slightly tongue-in-cheek. Indie magazine publishers may not have deep pockets, but they do need unlimited credit when it comes to tenacity and determination.

If you're still reading, you might just have what it takes …

5. *The Gourmand*, issue 1, December 2012

6. *Gratuitous Type*, issue C, 2013

7. *IdN*, volume 21, number 3, 2014

8. *Delayed Gratification*, issue 1, October–December 2010

1.

Interview
The Publisher

Jefferson Hack
Editor-in-Chief, *Dazed & Confused*,
AnOther, *AnOther Man*; Founder,
Dazed Group

Even in its earliest incarnation – a folded poster launched in 1991 by the teenagers Jefferson Hack and Rankin Waddell – *Dazed & Confused* had serious attitude. It has evolved from ambitious upstart to serious player, always maintaining a maverick stance. Jefferson Hack has developed *Dazed* into a small but successful independent empire, including *Dazed Digital*, *AnOther* and *AnOther Man*. Few figures in the independent publishing world can match his experience and insight.

2.

What was the motivation for the first issue of *Dazed & Confused*?

There was a pre-*Dazed* magazine moment called *Untitled*. It was a student magazine that Rankin and I, and a colleague, Ian Taylor, were involved with. Rankin was at the London College of Printing [LCP], where I was [studying journalism], and he was doing a sabbatical as the student union communications officer. He had this vision that all the art colleges of the London Institute, which LCP was a part of [along with Saint Martin's School of Art, Chelsea School of Art, the Central School of Art and Design and Camberwell School of Arts and Crafts] should have a magazine that was distributed through all the colleges.

Rankin was recruiting people to help on this project, and I was the only one who turned up to the first meeting … I was the only willing victim. He said: 'Do you know who Gilbert and George are?' I said 'No.' He said: 'Oh, because they're Britain's most famous artists. You're interviewing them tomorrow morning and I'm taking the pictures.' And that was our first commission together – the beginning of our working relationship. It was that quick, we met one day and the next day we were on a job together.

I remember getting the first issue of that magazine back from the printer and feeling this very, very powerful sense of elation, a high, from having in my hand the physical copy of what had just been an idea. It seemed incredibly satisfying as a process – that buzz, the first one, is the one I've been chasing ever since.

Did you always want to make magazines?

Yes, I've always been a magazine junkie; I've always collected them: magazines like *Interview*, *Oz*, old copies of independent press titles that weren't going any more that I came across in thrift shops. I loved *MAD* magazine as a kid, but *Interview* was particularly important for me. It was my first conscious experience of being transported from living in an English seaside town, Ramsgate, and being able to access New York club culture – to feel connected to a certain culture that wasn't around me but was in the magazine, the ability to get that information and that perspective, the writing, the editing, the package, the way that world was coming alive in the magazine. That stuff wasn't on television, there was no Internet; the magazine was the portal into that world. The power and energy of that were just too cool. That gave me a confidence and hope and connection that I really loved.

1. Jefferson Hack, portrait by Brantley Gutierrez

2. The first issue of *Dazed & Confused* (1991) was a folded-poster format

I was 19 when I started *Dazed*. We were very young. We didn't care about anything, didn't care about money, eating, family, anything, apart from enjoying what we were doing and doing something meaningful that we couldn't do at college or in a professional capacity. So this idea of interviewing people and creating a fanzine, or a hybrid between a poster magazine and a fanzine, was a way of connecting the dots about what was going on in the culture at the time.

It didn't come from a place of business plans or 'gaps in the market' … We were the readers and we were making it for ourselves and our friends, and we had a particular attitude because we were part of what was happening in London in the early 1990s, which was particularly explosive. It became an internationally recognized thing, and we had all these people around us doing amazing things, so it became a platform for that expression.

3.

Was there a moment when you realized *Dazed* was moving from a fanzine to something different?

There were a couple of key shifts. One was when we went from a poster magazine to being stapled. A complete shift in format, a complete shift in perception.

Also, the first celebrity cover we did, with Björk, was amazing because we'd never worked with musicians or other celebrities before. It felt as though we were growing up because a star had called the magazine. I answered the phone, and she said: 'This is Björk. I really like your magazine, can we do something together?' I was really shocked. That was a transitional moment. I realized that something was going on, that people were starting to respect what we did and could see we had a point of view, and wanted to participate in and collaborate with that.

I think another shift was when Bill Clinton said in a speech [in 1997] that *Dazed & Confused*, among some other titles he name-checked, was responsible for 'heroin chic'. As a result of that, the current issue of *Dazed* sold out. We got another issue out super-quick, printed as many as we could afford and built our circulation very, very quickly – it put another zero on our circulation. It was phenomenal.

The next defining moment happened in that same period: the Alexander McQueen 'Fashion Able' cover, with the sprinter Aimee Mullins [the Paralympic gold medallist, shot for *Dazed* in 1998], that Lee [McQueen] art-directed, Nick Knight photographed and Katy England styled. When that came out it was in nearly every national paper. It was pretty global, from America to South Africa to France, and it went viral; it was a big media story at the time. That was the point when we felt we'd

3. *Dazed & Confused*, issue 46, 1996, Aimee Mullens, concept by Alexander McQueen, photography by Nick Knight, styling by Katy England

4. *Dazed & Confused*, issue 16, featuring Björk, the magazine's first 'celebrity' cover star

become a magazine. We realized that it wasn't really about having the biggest audience or being the number-one seller, it was about being the best magazine and about the influence that you can have if you've got a good story … It was phenomenal, and set quite a bit of debate going over the stigma felt by disabled people and how society treats others. It was a very healthy debate to have, and it was that cover that sparked the debate.

You added the biannual title *AnOther*, which launched in 2001, a second biannual title, *AnOther Man* (in 2005), and the whole digital publishing side. Has that been a natural evolution?

Dazed was about ten years old when *AnOther* was launched. *AnOther* was started for a number of reasons, but mainly because there was a new generation coming through in the team at *Dazed*. There was an existing generation, including Katy England and Alister Mackie and me, and some editors. The problem was that with the new photographers, writers and stylists coming through, there were just not enough pages – everyone was fighting for pages each month. People were starting to feel that they didn't have a voice, that they had to wait in the queue to have a feature published.

Another important thing for me at the time was that with *Dazed* I felt as though I was pressing the fast-forward button all the time – everything was about speed and acceleration. I wanted to do a magazine on a different frequency and have longer stories. The main thing was the time frame: the fashion industry and the advertising cycle around fashion suited the formula of a biannual.

How do you approach relationships with advertisers? Your independence means you can do things your way, but you also have a very successful relationship with the industry. Is that ever problematic?

I think you have to deliver. You're only really as good as your last set of issues. You have to keep innovating, keep delivering. You have to remain relevant and prove yourself from season to season. It's been a long, long process of getting noticed, getting accepted, getting some advertisers, retaining the relationships, building on those relationships. Nothing for me has happened overnight. It was ten years of *Dazed* and then it was five years of *AnOther* before it split and went to be *AnOther Man*. That's the entire lifespan of many magazines. It's a lifetime in the digital era. You build trust and relationships, but it takes a long time and there's no magic formula.

4.

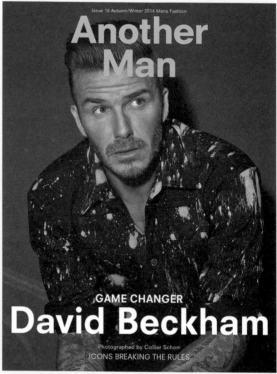

5.

6.

Do you ever say 'no' to advertisers?

To be honest, it's all about context. Most advertisers who aren't appropriate for us don't want to be in our environment by virtue of our rate card and our position. Online, there's a lot of inappropriate advertising, but we have a very high CPM ['cost per mille', the cost of an advertisement per 1,000 views] to avoid that. We don't do automatic advertising, we only do direct sales, so nothing gets in that hasn't come through the system. And if it doesn't look good and the creative is bad, we're on to them and we say: 'This is not going to work, you have to do something about this. If you really want to excite our readers, you've got to change the creative, or we'll help you.'

Is your *Dazed Digital* audience different from that of the print magazine?

It's bigger and the gender is less female. Print is probably 80 per cent female, and online is more like 65 per cent.

How do you make people stay on your website and keep coming back?

It's the power of the story and how you tell it. We have different frequencies of story-telling; not everything has to be short to win on the web. A lot of the metrics are changing, and what we look at is engagement, not hits. We look at time on site and the interactivity we get, like commenting, which means readers are emotionally engaged with a story and are likely to 'share' or 'like' it. Engagement is much more important to us than just the top-line figure of how many people landed on a page.

So we're moving from what we call the 'click web' to the 'attention web'. I'm very interested in that from a story-teller's perspective – the change in how we measure behaviour and quantify it. I want to understand people's total attention, not just where they're clicking.

We're in the early days. It's going to evolve; there's much more beauty to emerge from what's happening online. Print has been around for a very, very long time. It's only really in the independent sector that anything interesting is happening in print. You really, really have to push it now to do anything that's interesting or modern-feeling, because most of the best work in print was done in the 1960s and '70s and most of what happens now is a copy of that. I see very little in print now that's new, and when I do see it, it's in the independent press because that's where people are taking the time and passion and putting the work into doing it. But on the web I see it every day.

What has being independent allowed you to do?

I don't know any other way than independent, so I couldn't tell you in a comparative sense. But what I do know is that no one tells me what to do. And collectively, therefore, no one tells us what to do, because I'm really only an extension of a team. I really mean that.

Being independent means you can't pass the buck. When you're working in a way that's that emotional, you're not driven by data or protocol – it's emotional decision-making. That's another definition of independence for me. It means you feel really shit about yourself a lot of the time because you think 'I could do better,' or 'I should have done that.' You can't pass the buck, you've only got yourself to rely on.

What advice would you give a fledgling independent magazine publisher?

Get a great name, one that you can copyright or trademark. And get a great team. Work with your own peer group rather than people with experience: it's much better to have the same set of references and the same kind of taste.

Make sure you have a digital component, or, in fact, nowadays I would say be digital first in your thinking. If you're in the indie sector you can be a print-only publication, but it depends what your ambition is. Digital is where the conversation is, if you want to be commercially relevant.

Finally, be more than a magazine. The editorial statement of the first issue of *Dazed* said: 'This is not a magazine,' and we really meant that. *Dazed* is a movement, and only a small percentage of the actions we do ever end up in print. That's what I believe has given *Dazed* its longevity, because it's more than a magazine; it has a purpose – to empower youth culture – that's bigger than the sum of its parts.

5. *AnOther*, issue 27, 2014.
Kate Moss, photography by Collier Schorr, styling by Katy England

6. *Another Man*, issue 19, 2014.
David Beckham, photography by Collier Schorr, styling by Alister Mackie

Choose your
own adventure

02

Build your publishing
model

Goals and ambitions

Define your
magazine's vital
statistics

Planning a publishing model

Planning a magazine means making a series of decisions, the outcome of which will determine both the tangible and intangible characteristics of your title. To get these elements right means that you need to think about your magazine as an object at the same time as you devise your publishing model.

Sit down with your team, collaborators or a trusted friend or advisor, and work through the ideas and checklists in this chapter. There are case studies giving working examples of different approaches to various aspects of the publishing model, and you will find lots more information about all the topics, including help with making the important decisions, throughout the book.

You definitely don't want to find yourself in debt for having a great time making something. Therefore, you need a practical and realistic approach to moulding a sustainable publishing model that can pay for itself. Follow the steps in this chapter to craft the building blocks of your title.

For a lot of indie publishers, their magazine can't pay them a full-time living wage; it's a passion project carried out at evenings and weekends, or something they can piggy-back on to their other work as writers, designers or photographers. Indeed, it may well be a showcase for their talents and a driver for new business. For these publishers, the motivation is not directly about making money, it's about the three Cs: creativity, collaboration and communication. Having the opportunity to put something brilliant together, work on it with amazingly talented people and get it out to an audience is all the payment they need.

Other publishers, while prizing independence, want the term to be synonymous not with hobbyism, but with a serious money-making venture. For them, the aim is a fully self-sustaining model that pays for wages and office space, and even shows a profit. At a debate between publishers at the independent publishing conference IndieCon 2014 in Hamburg, Kati Krause reported for MagCulture that the founder of *The Weekender* magazine, Dirk Mönkemöller, said: 'I don't want to be able to make a living from the magazine … I might have to do things that I don't want to, and I'd fear for its soul.' On the other hand, Katarzyna Mol-Wolf, publisher of the magazines *Emotion* and *Hohe Luft*, said: 'I want my magazines to be bought and to pay my bills. I don't want to do indie and die indie.' This debate represents two sides to independent publishing.

Where do your ambitions lie?

1.

"You need to be passionate and a little crazy."

Felix Burrichter, *PIN-UP*

1. Addressing the audience, IndieCon 2015

"Make something you're comfortable with."

Simon Esterson, *Eye*

2.

3.

Vital statistics

The way you structure the logistical and financial side of your magazine is just as important as how it will look and read. Sketching out the numbers is the first step in a lot of big decisions, and is bound up with choices about how you'll produce the physical object.

It is sensible to start with a clear plan, even if it is modest in scale; you can always adapt and develop it later. As you determine the basics, such as print run, frequency and revenue streams, each piece of the jigsaw will help you to place the next.

If you're starting small, with your own money, take baby steps. If you mean to launch with an ambitious statement of a magazine, be prepared to plan in excruciating detail and get investment. At one end of the spectrum, you might be printing 500 copies of a 32-page A4 (or 8½ x 11 inch) stapled magazine to send to blog readers or members of your club twice a year. At the other end is a monthly magazine printing 100,000 copies, to be sold in bookshops and newsagents around the world, carrying advertising from high-end global brands. Most indie magazines sit somewhere between these poles.

'I don't think there's any shame in starting by making 1,000 copies of something – you don't have to do the finished product straight up,' says Will Hudson of *It's Nice That*. 'Do a newspaper to show an editorial tone, get it out and into people's hands, then see if it leads to something.'

See *Wrap* case study on page 58

Wrap magazine, now in its fifth year, began life as a newsprint publication, only evolving into today's format of a 104-page perfect-bound magazine once its makers, Polly Glass and Chris Harrison, had built up a following of readers. 'The spec was pretty lo-fi for the first edition, compared to how *Wrap* looks today,' says Glass, 'which made it relatively affordable to test it out as an idea, and see how people would react. Luckily the concept was really well received, and so from there on, the magazine has been able to support itself.'

2. *Wrap*, issue 1, 2010

3. *Wrap*, issue 10, 2014

What's the plan? Your publishing blueprint

Ask yourself	Consider	Consult
How many copies will you print?	**Your market and your budgets.** Realistically, how many people will buy each issue? How many can you afford to print, and how will you sell them? **Crowdsourced funding or online pre-sales** can help you to determine how many you need to print. **If you plan to carry advertising**, you need volume to attract brands.	**Your printer** for costing options. **Your distributor,** if you'll be using one, on what volume they can place with retailers. **Chapter 8** on financial planning. **Page 144** on defining a print run. **Chapter 7** about getting advertisers. **Potential advertisers** about their expectations.
How often will the magazine be published?	**Will you be monthly, bimonthly, quarterly, biannual or annual, etc.?** Think about how much time you can commit, the type of content you have, the community you represent and how your readers want to consume the magazine. Frequency is crucial to costs and revenue.	**Chapter 8** for advice on cash flow. **Pages 30–31** for a guide to magazine frequency. **Other magazines** in the market.
Will you carry advertising?	**Think about your market.** Are there enough brands that will advertise? How will you compete with the other magazines in the market? Will you make editorial concessions to your sponsors? Can you afford to reach your goals without advertising revenue?	**Chapter 7** on advertising. **Brands:** try to gauge interest from potential advertisers. **Other magazines:** make an audit of the number and type of ads in competing titles.
How will it be distributed?	**How much time and energy you can invest.** Can you handle distribution yourself? **If you're carrying advertising** you will want to maximize volume. This will probably make a distributor essential.	**Chapter 6** on distribution. **Pages 96–97** on DIY selling. **Distribution companies** about what they offer.
What's the cover price?	**Don't pluck it from the air.** How much do you need to charge to cover costs? What will people be prepared to pay? How much of your business model will rely on copy sales revenue?	**The market:** what are other magazines charging? **Your distributor,** if you're using one: what percentage of the cover price will end up in your pocket, and when will you get paid?

Easy rider versus the professionals

The Ride Journal

Frequency: About once a year
Print run: 5,000–6,000
Cover price: £8
Funding for launch:
Crowdsourced
Number of full-time staff: None
(part-time editor and part-time
art director)

Born out of brothers Andrew
and Philip Diprose's passion for
cycling, *The Ride Journal* is a
part-time pleasure for its makers,
showcasing the work of illustrators
and photographers and telling
stories about cyclists' experiences.
They explain: 'We figured out what
the printing cost was and then sold
enough advertising to pay for the
print run – all from people we've
known through bike races, shops
and friends. We went to them and
said, "Do you want to buy a page?
It's £400." Enough people said
"Yes," and we got our print-run
money. So now the adverts pretty
much pay for the printing costs, and
all the profit we make from sales
after distribution goes to charity.'

Disegno

Frequency: Biannual
Print run: 20,000–30,000
Cover price: £8
Funding for launch: Personal loan
and savings
Number of full-time staff: Eight

Launched in 2011, Disegno is a
more-than-full-time business for its
founder, Johanna Agerman Ross.
She saw a gap in the market for a
design title modelled on fashion
publishing, with two seasonal
issues a year, funded through
advertising relationships with high-
end brands. Revenue comes from
copy sales, advertising, events
and a studio that produces content
and editorial services for brands.
'Advertising is something that's
developing and becoming stronger
issue on issue,' she says. 'We
were lucky that, from issue 3, Saint
Laurent came to us wanting to
advertise. It meant a lot, because
their interest confirmed what I had
set out to do: to make a design
magazine that carried fashion
advertising.'

Surf's up versus knuckle down

Acid

Frequency: Every 6–9 months
Location: France
Print run: 2,000–3,000
Cover price: €12
Number of pages: 144

Turning up in a slightly unpredictable fashion, much like the surf itself, surfing magazine *Acid* is a passion project, standing for (in the words of its editor, Olivier Talbot) 'beauty, ideas, fun'. To print and ship the launch issue cost €4,400, most of which was covered by advertising sales. Issue-to-issue, revenue comes from copy sales (65 per cent) and advertising (35 per cent). 'We like to think of the publication as an exhibition,' says Talbot, 'where bits of contemporary culture are tied together by a link to surfing … It's super-good fun to run a project over which you have full control … None of us is getting paid.'

Lucky Peach

Frequency: Quarterly
Location: United States
Print run: 100,000
Cover price: $12
Number of pages: 172

The food-writing journal *Lucky Peach* began life under the aegis of indie US book publisher McSweeney's, becoming a stand-alone independent in 2013. As well as copy sales, revenue comes from advertising sales, both in print and online. At the time of writing, there were ambitions to publish a series of books and to launch *Lucky Peach* television. The magazine's approach to distribution is 'wherever we can', and it uses several distribution companies to supply bookshops and news-stands. Its publisher, Adam Krefman, says he counts increasing advertising revenue as one of the magazine's greatest triumphs.

Object analysis

If you're making a printed magazine, you need to define its shape and size. Consider not only the aesthetic implications of the dimensions and thickness of your magazine, but also what they will mean for your costs. Speak to your printer about the most economical dimensions and extent (number of pages). Think about how the object will best work as a vehicle for the content.

Your method of distribution might affect the size and shape. Ask yourself whether it is more important that your magazine is economical to post, or that it stands out on retailers' shelves, and consider that you may have to live with these early decisions for a long time.

See *Printed Pages* case study on page 82

Will Hudson, founder of INT Works and publisher of *It's Nice That* (2009–12) and *Printed Pages* (2013–) recalls the process of learning and discovery that he and his team went through in refining the publishing model of their first magazine, *It's Nice That*, to create its successor, *Printed Pages*. In the magazine's earliest incarnation, he admits that they were hung up on nice papers and high production values at the expense of economic sustainability. The number of copies and advertising pages they had to sell to meet their costs created so much pressure that they stopped publishing altogether.

After a break they returned to the drawing board, stripped back the model and devised a new title. 'When we launched *Printed Pages* in March 2013,' says Hudson, 'the magazine had broken even before we even sold a copy. We'd pared back those production values. We looked at the commissioning costs, we looked at the advertising and support that we could generate, and it was such a small number of issues [we needed] to sell that, as a studio, we got to celebrate the success of that issue almost immediately.'

"People challenging that status quo – I think that's where you get the most interesting results."

Will Hudson, *It's Nice That*

4. *It's Nice That*, issue 2, October 2009

5. *Printed Pages*, issue 1, Spring 2013

4.

5.

What shape and size? Right peg, right hole

Ask yourself	Consider	Consult
What size will the magazine be?	**What type of content are you showing?** A photography magazine showing lots of images needs more layout space than a poetry title.	**Chapter 4** for more about editorial design decisions. **Your designer** or **art director**.
	The economics of printing: some page dimensions will get more out of a sheet of paper.	**Pages 141–42** on printers and going to print. **Your printer**.
	Postage and packaging: How will the size affect delivery costs? What is the cost of sending magazines internationally? (Usually a lot.) Will you be posting copies yourself or using a fulfilment service and/or distribution company? Most postage services have cost thresholds based on size, weight and volume.	**Chapter 6** for all the different methods of getting your magazine out there. **The postal or fulfilment service** you will use about what they can offer.
How many pages will the magazine have?	**The pages** of any printed publication are imposed by the printer in 16-page sections. The most economical use of paper needs pages divisible by 16; the next best option is divisible by 8, then by 4.	**Your printer** for costs relating to paper quantities. **Pages 56–57** for more about flat plans and pagination. **Pages 136–39** for an interview with a print expert.
	What's your content? How many regular sections and features will you have, and how much space will you give them? Will the structure be fixed or change in each issue? Make a flat plan to nail down what goes where.	**Chapter 4** about editorial decision-making and flat plans.
	Your budget: how much paper can you afford? Your income per issue will determine how much you can spend making it.	**Chapter 8** about costing and cash flow.
How will it be bound?	**Saddle-stitched, perfect-bound or sewn?** There are many ways to hold the pages of your magazine together, but they may depend on the number of pages and the type of paper used.	**Your printer** for what binding services it supplies.
	How much it costs: fancy binding can be very expensive.	**Your printer** for binding costs. **Your designer**.

What's the frequency?

Episodic publishing has been around in various forms for centuries, but digital technology and online reading habits have changed the landscape completely in the last decade, with the Internet and social media outstripping the news function of periodicals. How often you put out an issue of your magazine could depend on the size of your operation. Weeklies and monthlies are largely the preserve of the commercial publishing world, where big teams and logistical staff shared across titles can accommodate a relentless publishing schedule. Smaller, self-sufficient, independent operations tend not to have the resources, in terms of both people-power and cash, to put out a magazine more than four times a year.

Decisions about frequency, however, are not entirely based on resources. They might also be linked to the industry or community you represent, the classic example being fashion publishing, which since 2000 has spawned a legion of biannual titles, timed to coincide with the well-entrenched fashion-industry seasons of Spring/Summer and Autumn/Winter.

Frequency is also affected by your editorial standpoint: making a statement at defined points through the year might be part of your editorial DNA. *The Gentlewoman*'s continued success and growth means that it could easily publish more often than twice a year, if numbers were all that mattered. But being biannual is essential to its editorial identity. 'I think our purpose is to offer a timely, quality opinion that stands out from the sea of constant content,' says its editor-in-chief, Penny Martin. 'When you feel you're surrounded by non-stop noise, it's important to be definitive, clear and editorially precise.' Likewise, the editorial concept of *Delayed Gratification* hinges on its quarterly frequency. 'We provide an alternative to the 24-hour news cycle and its preoccupation with breaking news by covering news with the benefit of three months'-worth of hindsight,' explains its associate editor, Matthew Lee. 'We aim to give new perspectives on stories the rest of the media covered, and to tell readers about stories the rest of the media missed.'

Read a full interview with Penny Martin on page 46–51

Print magazines are no longer the hungry reader's only connection to ideas, trends and information, as they were in the pre-Internet age. They have begun to settle into a slower pace, closer to that of books, balancing book-like production values with the time and change-marking qualities of periodical publishing. 'There are more biannuals and also more and more titles changing from quarterly to biannual,' observes the magazine retailer Marc Robbemond. 'It has to do with money and time: people often have jobs next to their magazine to support.

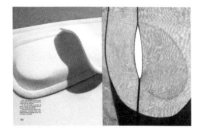

6.

7.

8.

The most important thing is to have consistent quality.'

When you publish a title twice a year it can become something of an event, and you can build anticipation, publicity and fanfare around each launch to help promote sales. 'We find that when we first launch something new there's a lot of support from the design and art community, promoting it and talking about it,' says Will Hudson of *It's Nice That*. 'But when you do something four times a year, there's less of a story. If you do it twice a year there's that much more weight to it, and more anticipation.'

Those making biannual magazines can invest book-like levels of attention in both editorial and design features. 'I like creating objects that are intriguing, that you can't ignore,' says *Noon*'s editor-in-chief, Jasmine Raznahan. 'The frequency allows each issue to be treated slightly differently, which means a new set of explorations into spot colours, foils, debossing, inserts, paper stocks, binding and typography'.

The biannual frequency also suits magazines with small teams who have to multitask. At the time of writing, several independent titles were about to make the switch from quarterly to biannual, including *Port*, *Cereal* and *The Carton*. In each case, the decision hinged on making fewer issues per year, allowing the team to invest more time in pushing their editorial offering to the next level, publish more pages per issue and source even better content. Needless to say it also means reducing your annual production and distribution costs.

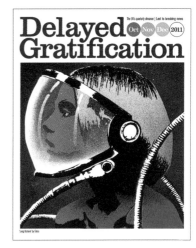

9.

10.

Get it out there

Try to tackle the daunting subject of distribution as early as possible. There is nothing more demoralizing for a publisher than to make a beautiful magazine full of amazing content only for it to sit, unread, in boxes. Deciding how you will offer your magazine to readers is an essential part of your business model. For this you need a clear idea of the revenues you can expect from different methods of distribution, but you must also understand something about your readers and how they consume things. Some magazines can access a ready market just by selling online; others need shelf-presence in shops to tempt customers. Even simple things, like where you will store the magazines after they arrive from the printer and how you will deliver them to customers, need serious thought.

Turn to chapter 6 for a detailed look at distribution

6. *The Gentlewoman*, issue 9, Spring/Summer 2014, spread from 'Pocket' feature, photography by Maurice Scheltens & Liesbeth Abbenes, styling by Sam Logan

7. *The Gentlewoman*, issue 8, Autumn/Winter 2013, 'Breakfast' article opener, photography by Maurice Scheltens & Liesbeth Abbenes

8. *The Gentlewoman*, issue 2, Autumn/Winter 2010, cover featuring Inez van Lamsweerde, photographed by Inez and Vinoodh

9. *Delayed Gratification*, issue 5, October–December 2011

10. *Delayed Gratification*, issue 11, April–June 2013, article on Moldovan children growing up without parents

Something of a rarity in the world of independent publishing, *Disegno* achieved early commercial success to the extent of paying for its own office and full-time staff of eight within three years. It operates as part of a small two-magazine publishing venture and creative studio, Tack Press. Here, Agerman Ross reveals how meticulous planning, foresight about publishing trends and sympathetic appreciation for commercial partners have built a rock-solid base for her magazine business.

1.

What's the publishing model for *Disegno*?

I can't claim that it's in any way revolutionary, because it's supported by advertising, but I guess what I wanted to do differently was inspired by what I saw in the fashion biannual. There was a hunger from luxury brands to place their ads in nice-looking magazines twice a year. I didn't feel the design magazine market had really clocked that.

I had been frustrated, in my previous role at *Icon*, that, editorially, fashion was a sideline. I always wanted it to be an equal part of looking at design. I saw *Disegno* as a chance for a more in-depth take on fashion writing.

In terms of business, I saw a niche. Just in 2014, three new design biannuals launched, so I guess *Disegno* has shown the way somehow. None are published by big publishing houses – all are independent – but it's interesting that we have set a format that has been looked at by other people.

Interview
The Start-up

Johanna Agerman Ross
Founder and Editor-in-Chief,
Disegno

How did you fund the launch of *Disegno*?

The funding was made up of my own savings and a personal loan from a friend from my schooldays, whom I paid back after a year. But I also worked really hard on paper and print sponsorship, and I asked contributors to write and photograph for free in exchange for getting them to places – I paid for the trips to cover the stories I wanted in the magazine.

How important are partnerships with suppliers for paper and print?

I felt paper and print were very important, and [that it was crucial] for me as publisher and founder of the business to be very involved with those things and have an understanding of what they mean for the mag. We worked with Fedrigoni paper from the start. For me that was really important, and I took a long time over finding a paper company that I could have a good relationship with. It took me the best part of a year from leaving *Icon* to set up those relationships. It's been really good to have discussions with Fedrigoni, evaluating after each issue to see how they think it looks. It has always been a part-sponsorship: we have always paid [for the paper] but maybe not the full price. And we always do other things with them. It's a good working relationship. We were sensitive to what they were interested in promoting. That relationship with Fedrigoni was a good foundation to start [the magazine] with.

1. Johanna Agerman Ross, photograph by Ivan Jones

2. *Disegno* issue 6, feature 'Seeing Through', photography by Ina Jang

White embellished plastic coat and ivory satin side pleats slip by Simone Rocha.

Seeing Through

Transparency in fashion is not always about straightforward exposure. It can reveal as much about the designer as it does the body beneath the clothes.

WORDS Tamsin Blanchard
PHOTOS Ina Jang

2.

What part does your online platform, *Disegno Daily*, play in your publishing?

I decided that if we did a biannual, there would be more opportunity to build a website and keep that as a talking point, a place for discussion and for keeping up to date with things. I always felt that the website and magazine had to be connected.

Another thing I added to the model was the events series. We have been doing talks and film screenings and tours, all kinds of things – trying to be inventive.

I felt if I started something new I wouldn't want to do the magazine first and then build the other things around it. It was important to do everything at the same time, otherwise you get into a routine. A magazine is a time-consuming thing, so you could find yourself asking 'How am I ever possibly going to add anything more to it?' I thought, if you start as you intend to go on and perfect everything later, that's a good way of doing it.

I remember the first document I wrote in Autumn 2010 (we launched in Autumn 2011) set out three focuses: not just fashion, design and architecture, but the three elements – live format, printed format, online format. They have been there from the beginning.

3.

What's your print run and how do you distribute the magazine?

We print 20,000–30,000 magazines. We have started being stocked by Barnes & Noble in the States, and they place a fairly big print order because they have so many stores. So [the circulation] has recently gone up. That's also an effect of having a sales team who have been working on expanding our distribution reach. Comag is our distributor; it's the muscle, as in it ships the magazine places, but then we also have an independent agent that works to promote *Disegno* to places like Barnes & Noble or a bookstore in Japan, or wherever.

For the first year and a half it was very frustrating. We were literally seen only in the places we contacted ourselves, and that's very time-consuming. I was calling people and going to see people, getting the magazine out whenever I travelled somewhere, making sure I always had copies with me. We still do that to an extent, but now we are happy that 100 per cent of the copies we print are out there.

What are your other distributor channels? Have you gone down the WHSmith route?

From Autumn 2014 we have been in WHSmith Travel – at airports and train stations. That WHSmith order was another big addition to our print run, so we're expanding both in the UK and internationally.

We've had a big readership in the US since the beginning, through our website. Actually, our first subscribers came from the US, so we know there is a big magazine-hungry audience there, but we still don't feel we've reached enough places. As well as Barnes & Noble, we also have stores like McNally Jackson in the middle of Soho in New York, which seems to be selling our magazine very well.

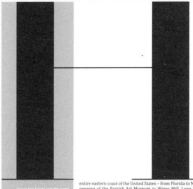

The central spine runs the length of the building with the galleries flanking it.

entire eastern coast of the United States – from Florida to Maine – four days before the planned opening of the Parrish Art Museum in Water Mill, Long Island, New York. As a result, on 2 November 2012, instead of a gathering of patrons, local artists and the museum's architects and designers, there was the whirr of an emergency generator, a handful of security guards and a museum director with a worried and tired look in her eyes, wondering when the electricity would start working again.

At least the building remained intact, having withstood the hurricane force winds and the debris it swept along with it. Sandy was the museum's second hurricane in as many years and the building is subject to a stringent hurricane code[2]. "Scientists have been awaiting the hurricane cycle for a while and now it's starting, so this was a reminder of why the code is in place," says Terrie Sultan, the Parrish Art Museum director.

It's an overcast autumn day, but despite the cloud coverage the light is painfully bright as I step from the car outside the Museum. The light is one of the reasons why this place, the East End of Long Island[3], has become such a popular destination for artists since the Long Island Railroad extended its services to Southampton in 1870[4]. The East End is only two hours from Manhattan, and the stream of artists heading there has never stopped, starting with the founder of American Impressionism William Merritt Chase[5], who established a school for plein-air painting[6] here in 1891, and continuing with Fairfield Porter[7], Jackson Pollock[8], Lee Krasner[9], Willem de Kooning[10] and Roy Lichtenstein[11]. Even the contemporary art scene pays attention to the East End, with people like Ross Bleckner[12], Eric Fischl[13], Chuck Close[14] and Elizabeth Peyton[15] establishing studios in the area. It is this long list of artists and their relationship to the location that has made the new incarnation of the Parrish Art Museum possible. And yet, for a while, it looked like it wouldn't happen at all.

The Parrish Art Museum was established in 1898 by the wealthy lawyer Samuel Longstreth Parrish[16] in Southampton, 10 minutes by car from Water Mill. Parrish's museum housed a collection of Italian Renaissance paintings, as was a la mode for the wealthy at the time. Although he donated some of the land for the establishment of Chase's Shinnecock Hills Summer School of Art, he never collected art by his contemporaries. It wasn't until the 1950s, with the donation of a collection of American paintings by the then president of the museum's board Rebecca Bolling Littlejohn, that the museum adopted the focus it has today: modern and contemporary American art from the local area. "We are a regional museum and we are very proud of the region, because who hasn't worked here?" asks Sultan rhetorically as she walks through the echoing, new museum. The galleries are not yet completely installed and there is a beauty to the half-unpacked crates – some paintings still under wraps, others leaning >

72 Disegno. PARRISH ART MUSEUM

PARRISH ART MUSEUM Disegno. 73

4.

3. *Disegno*, issue 3, 2012, image by Ola Bergengren

4. *Disegno*, issue 4, 2013, feature on Parrish Art Museum, photography by Janette Beckman

Do you have more news-stand buyers or subscribers?

It's definitely a bigger percentage who buy it from the news-stand, I think because it's a biannual. There's a bigger need to have a subscription with a monthly magazine, because you feel you miss out on something, whereas with a biannual it's more desirable to go [to a shop] and buy it. We have institutions who subscribe – museums and schools and so on – and companies. We have seen an increase in that type of subscriber.

Was the advertising side of the business difficult to get going, and has it changed?

The relationship with advertisers has to be constantly massaged, entertained and looked after. There's an age-old dilemma: a lot of magazines feel that if they carry advertising they have to pander to the advertisers to some degree. That's something we've been very careful not to do as a magazine. We have our editorial stance and we see that as quite separate, and advertising is something that complements our content. I have always seen advertising as a valuable part of the magazine because I personally think it's nice to look at advertising in a magazine, if it's well done. Sadly, this is where the design industry is very far behind the fashion industry, where they invest significant budgets in making very interesting, beautiful campaigns every season. But in the design industry, you often see [a brand] having the same art for at least a year, sometimes more. That's not as inspirational as going through the September issue of *Vogue*.

How did you arrive at your cover price? You get a lot of magazine for £8.

We used to be £15, but we brought the price down because of the international market. It's very difficult to control the price of the magazine abroad, because of the different tax settings. In the UK there is no tax on printed products, but in Europe it can be anything from 6 to 25 per cent, so the price for which the magazine sells can vary a lot. If it costs something like €35, no one is going to buy it, so bringing the cover price down was a way of being able to expand distribution.

Although it might hurt immediately, in the long term it means that you build a broader distribution base, which is obviously what you want to do as a magazine.

What have been the key moments in *Disegno*'s evolution?

The first was when we realized we were outgrowing our kitchen – we got to the point where there was just no more space. It was also about having a healthy life; it was either being in front of your desk or in bed, no in-between times. Looking at our finances and realizing we could afford an office was a really big moment. It was always something we thought we could skimp on, but to come to the conclusion that we could actually afford it – but also needed it – and to leave the house and go to work on the first day, was a good moment.

There's also a moment when you realize you can relinquish control. I used to clean the office myself every week. It was only a few months ago that we realized, actually, it would probably be more beneficial if we just paid someone to do it. That was significant.

5.

6.   7.   8.

5. *Disegno*, issue 5, 2013,
article on 101 Spring Street,
the studio and living space of
Donald Judd, photography by
Christopher Patrick Kent

6. *Disegno*, issue 4, 2013,
photograph by Ola Bergengren

7. *Disegno*, issue 5, 2013,
photograph by Giles Price

8. *Disegno*, issue 7, 2014,
illustration by Studio Olafur Eliasson

What questions should an aspiring magazine publisher ask themselves?

The one thing that everyone seems not to understand is how much time it takes. You need to ask yourself if you're up for the sacrifices it leads to. If you do want to start it as a business that's going to support you and the people you work with, it will be very, very time-consuming and you have to go through several years to get where you want to be.

On the other hand, it can be good not to ask the questions, to go in a bit blind. If someone had told me exactly what the process would be from when I started to now, I would probably have said: 'No, I'll stick to the day job.' But when you come out at the other end, it's very rewarding to see that you've made something that works and that you can support yourself and a team, and pay office rent and things like that. I would say, though, that you need a specific psyche – being quite stubborn. Both Marcus [Agerman Ross, Johanna's husband and partner in Tack Press] and I have benefited from not being able to take 'no' for an answer from anyone.

You need to be passionate about your subject matter. We're not business people: I come from a design history and writing background, and Marcus comes from styling and photography. But that has really helped us: everything in *Jocks and Nerds* is what he's passionate about through and through; everything in *Disegno* is something I can stand and shout about from the rooftops. If you don't have a true, passionate interest, then it's easy to give up when things don't go your way. To the point of being stupid, you have to believe in what you're doing.

Who's who?

Magazine teams,
contributors,
freelancers and
suppliers

Multitasking
magazine nomads

People power

Assembling the right team around you is one of the most important things you can do to sustain yourself as a magazine. It could be that you have a natural team of collaborators from the start, or you might have to seek out the right people to help you get your title out, make it look great and sell it. Whatever your size or set-up, a magazine team needs to be tight, because there will be late nights and difficult decisions. The key people making a magazine need to be on the same wavelength, with shared reference points and attitudes to work.

Several of the editors at the top of the independent magazine field say the same about what makes a good team: work with your own peer group, they say, and don't just seek people with an established name because you like what they've done before. It's about giving voice to your gang, writing about what you know and not just saying what you think people want to hear. 'The magazines I think are great are made by people who make them for themselves and their friends,' says Penny Martin, editor-in-chief of *The Gentlewoman*. 'That's not to say they're exclusive. They're just confident and specific in tone.'

Work with people you respect and can develop with: 'A good magazine is not one person's point of view,' says Jefferson Hack. 'A real, genuine magazine has to have a series of strong leaders and strong points of view. A really good editor-in-chief, a really good graphic designer, a really great photo editor: the three of them need to be at a similar level. If one is weak it lets the whole thing down; you're looking at it going, "Nice photography, shame about the words." All those elements need to be in synch.'

"It's to do with getting that magical integration of people and ideas right."

Dan Crowe, *Port*

Introducing the band

The masthead in a magazine is the page where you list everyone who is involved in making it. Sometimes this can run to legions of people (see *Monocle*'s) or just a handful (*Offscreen* is pretty much a one-man operation). There is a traditional line-up and hierarchy based on long-held publishing conventions, but increasingly, independent titles are working in new ways with smaller, more fluid teams. Jobs and responsibilities are less clearly defined, and people are responsible for work outside the traditional definitions of, say, 'publisher' and 'art director'. However big or small your operation, the masthead is the place to make sure all the people who have helped to make the magazine get their proper credit, and that any reader picking up your title can easily find names and contact details. It can be a very revealing page in any publication.

Read a full
interview with
Simon Esterson
and John
Walters on
pages 70–75.

Magazine-makers in the independent
sector are nimble, multitasking nomads,
roaming between their editorial roles and
other work. 'Indie mags mean a small, agile
team,' observes Simon Esterson of *Eye*,
who, along with editor John Walters, gets
on with jobs like ordering mailing boxes
and managing subscriptions promotions
as well as his main job of art-directing and
designing the magazine. Making a magazine
is about mucking in with every aspect of its
creation, manufacture and distribution.

Your team will wax and wane according
to where you are in the publishing schedule.
Teams swell with extra hands on deck during
the design phase, or when it comes to
processing orders once the issue is on sale.

"The most important thing is the people you surround yourself with."

Marta Puigdemasa, *Perdiz*

How many people work *part-time* on your core team?

0	1	2	3-5	6+
59%	14%	9%	12%	6%

How many people work *full-time* on your core team?

0	1	2	3-5	6+
9%	9%	34%	30%	18%

These charts give a breakdown of full- and part-time team
members for a sample of 34 independent magazines surveyed
for this book, with print runs ranging from 1,000 to 75,000 copies.
Of the 14 magazines that had any full-time staff, 11 used a
combination of full- and part-time team members. Well over half
the magazines that answered this question had no full-time staff
at all, and were run completely as part-time ventures (59 per cent).

1.

2.

3.

4.

5.

6.

1. Colin Caradec and Morgane Rébulard, editors, *The Shelf*

2. Polly Glass and Chris Harrison, editors, *Wrap*, with issue 8, photo by Lydia Garnett

3. *FUKT* team in action, photo by Björn Hedgard

4. *Perdiz* team from left to right: Eloi Montenegro, Marta Puigdemasa, Marc Sancho and Borja Ballbé; photo by Borja Ballbé and Querida Studio

5. Jessica Lowe and Gavin Green, editors, *Cat People*

6. Kai Brach, editor, *Offscreen*, photo by Nikita Helm

7.

8.

7. *Boat*, issue 8, 2014, Los Angeles

8. *Boat*, issue 9, 2015, Bangkok

9. *Port*, issue 9, Spring 2013, photography Stefan Ruiz, creative directors Matt Willey and Kuchar Swara

Read more about *Boat* on page 132

Boat magazine presents a unique experiment in magazine-making, assembling and dismantling a bespoke team in a new city for each issue.

As well as your core team, your magazine will depend on input from freelance contributors in the form of writing, proofreading, photography, illustration and design. Don't underestimate the importance of a reliable proofreader and the value of an extra pair of eyes checking your magazine before it goes to print; there is nothing more heartbreaking than getting an issue back from the printer to find that there's a devastating typo or you've got the spelling of someone's name wrong. You might be too wrapped up in the process to spot glaring mistakes.

Contributors, freelancers and suppliers

One of your greatest assets as a magazine is a roster of reliable, high-quality contributors. Find them, nurture them and treat them well. There is such a thing as publishing karma: the way you work with people comes through in the end product, and not honouring your relationships will come back to bite you. Be clear with freelancers from the start about the terms of your working relationship, and stay true to that. A lot of indie magazines swap favours with writers, illustrators and photographers, but make sure you deliver on your side of the bargain. When you're paying cash, even if the fees are small, pay on time. If you're really, really stuck and cash flow means you can't pay on time, keep talking. There is nothing worse than the silent treatment when you're a freelance contributor waiting for payment, and it's amazing what an apology and an honest explanation can do to save the situation.

When you're making an editorial budget, you need to decide how important high-quality paid-for writing is to your vision for the magazine. It might be your title's *raison d'être*, as with *Delayed Gratification*: 'We believe that quality journalism costs money, so we pay contributors and we plan to raise our word rate when we can afford to do so,' says Matthew Lee, the magazine's associate editor.

Rosa Park, the publisher of *Cereal*, has also worked a financial aspect into the magazine's editorial strategy and ethos: 'We're a travel magazine, so we're always on the road,' she says. 'We go to every single place that we feature, and we don't ever take freebies. We pay every single contributor. It's a costly affair for a business of our size.'

"The factory floor is being run by the workmen."

Kuchar Swara, *Port*

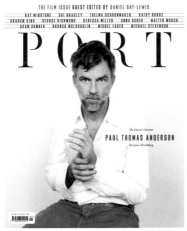

THE FILM ISSUE GUEST EDITED BY DANIEL DAY-LEWIS

RAY WINSTONE   DAI BRADLEY   THELMA SCHOONMAKER   KATHY BURKE
GRAHAM KING   GEORGE RICHMOND   REBECCA MILLER   ANNA SCHER   WALTER MURCH
ADAM SOMNER   BRONCO MCLOUGHLIN   MICHEL FABER   MICHAEL STEVENSON

PORT

The Master Detonator
PAUL THOMAS ANDERSON
By Lynn Hirschberg

9.

Read more in an interview with Johanna Agerman Ross on pages 32–37

Read *The White Review* case study on page 79

Developing relationships with contributors and suppliers who share your vision and ethics gets you some stability in an uncertain world and affects the reader's experience on every page. 'The last two years have taught me that it's very difficult to find people who understand exactly what you want to do and are on the same wavelength as you,' says Park. 'Once I have found those people, I have held on to them.'

'You've got to start right at the top, and that's why I poach writers from the *New Yorker*,' says Dan Crowe, editor-in-chief of *Port*. 'Dan's so classically good at convincing people who wouldn't do those sorts of things for other people,' rejoins his *Port* co-founder, Kuchar Swara. 'How do you get Daniel Day-Lewis to guest-edit an issue? How do you get Philip Seymour Hoffman on your cover when he hates all that stuff?' 'It's just conversations, it's being nice,' says Crowe.

Crowe might make feats of commissioning sound easy, but developing and nurturing your relationships with contributors is a crucial editorial function that requires finesse. Make sure your writers feel valued; after all, it's their words that will make the most impact in your magazine.

Choosing the right suppliers for print and paper and brokering mutually beneficial agreements can be a make-or-break factor in your business plan. If your title represents an opportunity to show off fine paper and high-quality print, you might get a reduced rate. Pick up the phone and talk to potential suppliers; go to meet them in person, and see how they work. It took Johanna Agerman Ross a year to find the right paper and print suppliers, but the sponsorship she got made her magazine *Disegno* financially viable from its launch. Such deals are a two-way street, so listen and be open-minded about what your potential partners are interested in promoting.

'The way to bring costs down is to develop personal and mutually beneficial relationships with people you're working with,' says Benjamin Eastham of *The White Review*. 'Then it becomes possible to make something that would otherwise be impossible. We have a very good relationship with our printer, Push, in Bermondsey. They have given us a very good deal from the start. They use the magazine as a showcase for what they can do.'

Singular visions, alternative lifestyles

Hole & Corner

Frequency: Biannual
Date launched: May 2013
Location: London
Print run: 10,000
Strapline: 'Celebrating craft, beauty, passion and skill'

'It's about people who spend more time "doing" than "talking", who put content above style, whose work is their life,' says *Hole & Corner*'s founder and creative director, Sam Walton. With a background in creative direction for high-end brands and as a designer at British *Vogue*, Walton combines his publishing project with creative and editorial services for brands. A real multitasker, he has a knack of bringing in world-class contributors, and applies the same attitude to publishing platforms: 'We aim to promote local trade and talented individuals, whether professional or amateur … with some of the world's finest still-life, style and fashion photographers, renowned film-makers and experienced producers.'

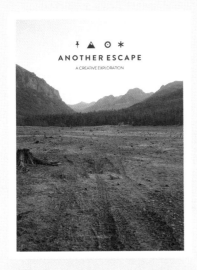

Another Escape

Frequency: Biannual
Date launched: April 2013
Location: Bristol
Print run: 8,000–10,000
Strapline: 'Outdoor lifestyle, creative culture and sustainable living'

Part of a new breed of lifestyle magazine that has sprung up since about 2010, *Another Escape* focuses on story-telling and on revealing the practices and lifestyles of interesting individuals. 'We are gentle and humble in tone, with an investigative nature,' say its founders, Rachel Taylor and Jody Daunton, whose backgrounds are in illustration and photography respectively. Both now work full-time on the magazine. Success has come from their willingness to jump headlong into multitasking: 'A very challenging aspect of creating an independent magazine is being able to switch between roles: you must be the business manager, the editor and the creative director rolled into one.'

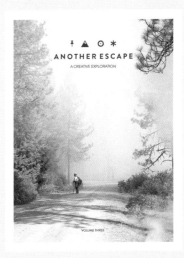

1.

Interview
The Editor in-Chief

Penny Martin
Editor-in-Chief,
The Gentlewoman

1. Penny Martin, photograph
by Ivan Jones

2. *The Gentlewoman*, issue 9,
Spring/Summer 2014, Vivienne
Westwood photographed by
Alasdair McLellan

The biannual women's magazine *The Gentlewoman* was launched in 2010 by the publisher of *Fantastic Man*. Defying conventions about women's magazines and fashion titles, it has carved out a unique place in the publishing firmament with intelligent, witty journalism, exemplary standards in design and photography, and a focus on real women's lives, rather than products and slavish adherence to commercial fashion cycles. At the helm is Penny Martin, a former academic, a curator and previously editor-in-chief of the pioneering fashion website SHOWstudio.

What's the starting point for an issue of *The Gentlewoman*?
There's a big editorial meeting, and then a lot of it happens by email. It's rare to have your fashion director [Jonathan Kaye], who shoots a lot in New York and Paris, in town at the same time as your creative director [Jop van Bennekom], and maybe also your deputy editor [Caroline Roux]. We're not like a monthly publication where there are scores of us, all in the office together. There's quite a lot of in-and-out. But one of the great advantages of our art director [Veronica Ditting, until recently based in Amsterdam] coming to live in London is that she and I can work a bit more closely. I think that is starting to change things already, which is really enjoyable.

What stage are you at with the next issue?
We go into production [for the Autumn/Winter issue] in mid-July, and we'll finish in the second week of August, so our artwork deadlines will be in early July and I'd like a lot of the interviews and bigger pieces by mid-June. But it's May, so we're nearing the time when I would like a cover confirmed. And I'm always in this state: everyone who knows me now just associates me with being in a complete flap about the cover. Covers are always difficult.

Is the cover the hardest bit?
Well, if I say 'the Beyoncé issue' or the 'Adele issue', that cover image comes to represent an entire six months of work – all ten interviews, seven essays and eight fashion stories. So it's a crucial symbol. Plus there's a long stretch of shelf life from one issue to the next, so you have to feel confident that you'll want to live through the production process with that cover, and then live through the following six months of it being on the news-stand and in the image at the foot of your email. It's the person you're constantly interviewed about; you end up having a really intimate relationship with the cover star, whether you personally interviewed her or not.

London

When
Vivienne
talks,
we
should
listen

Portraits by Alasdair McLellan   115

2.

You've achieved a few surprises and talking points with your covers. The Angela Lansbury cover [no. 6, Autumn/Winter 2012] is cited a lot for featuring an 86-year-old woman. Are you breaking expectations about fashion publishing?

Well, she'd been on my list since I first had my job interview, so it wasn't a case of 'Wow, wouldn't we capture media attention with her?' I just knew it would be a brilliant shoot. And it's great that she's been so much in the public imagination since the issue came out: she got her honorary Oscar [Academy Honorary Award, 2013], she got her damehood [Dame Commander of the Order of the British Empire 'for services to drama and to charitable work and philanthropy', 2014], she's been on in the West End [*Driving Miss Daisy*, 2013; *Blithe Spirit*, 2014]. It's been wonderful that we got mixed up with that late-career renaissance; it's been to our huge advantage. That image – you wouldn't believe the number of people who stop me to talk about it.

Adele was another turning point for us, because she really came to mass prominence around the time that third issue was out [Spring/Summer 2011], when her album sold all those millions of copies and she won big at the Brits. It really clarified our position on the whole plus-size topic, which was always going to be an issue for us, as a women's magazine, without us even having to acknowledge it. You know, we featured Adele and Angela because they're brilliant at what they do and they're really lovely women, not because of their size or age. But it's really nice to think that, rather than exploiting them to stage some phoney debate, those covers turned them into contemporary fashion icons.

You have certain carefully defined aspects visually and editorially in the structure of the magazine, but there is also evolution. How much was that intended from the start?

It's in the character of the people who work here that we never want to repeat things; if we have editorial formats, we don't want them to become too fixed. Some can be great, like the 'Modernisms' interviews at the beginning of the magazine. We ran those in the first two or three issues and then began to wonder if we should change that section, but we decided [not to], that they were our equivalent of shopping pages, except that they prioritized conversation over product. It's an important distinction.

There are components of a grid, but the magazine pretty much gets redesigned from scratch every time, when the assets come in. You can be far more experimental that way. And Jop and Veronica have very high standards. They come from a Dutch graphic-design background, which means their approach is very editorially led. I think it's rare to have art directors who find it necessary to understand and to some extent shape the editorial direction. And then they've got an editor who was very involved in photography [Martin was a curator at the National Museum of Photography, Film & Television, as well as working with Nick Knight on SHOWstudio]. It's a very luxurious situation, where we're able to step on one another's toes a little bit – it's not too departmental or territorial.

3. *The Gentlewoman*, issue 3, Spring/Summer 2011, Adele photographed by Alasdair McLellan

4. *The Gentlewoman*, issue 7, Spring/Summer 2013, Jekka McVicar photographed by Paul Wetherell

5. *The Gentlewoman*, issue 7, Spring/Summer 2013, 'Nice Things: Red Lipsticks', photography by Daniel Riera, styling by Sam Logan

3.

208

The pioneering herb farmer
from England

Jekka McVicar

209

4.

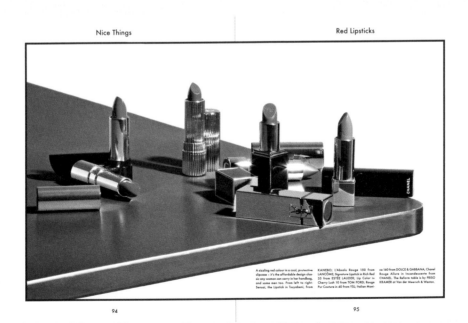

Nice Things

Red Lipsticks

A sizzling red colour is a cool, protective
slipcase – it's the affordable design clas-
sic any woman can carry in her handbag,
and some men too. From left to right:
Sensai, the Lipstick in Tsuyabeni, from
KANEBO; L'Absolu Rouge 130 from
LANCÔME; Signature Lipstick in Rich Red
35 from ESTÉE LAUDER; Lip Color in
Cherry Lush 10 from TOM FORD; Rouge
Pur Couture in 40 from YSL; Italian Moni-
ca 160 from DOLCE & GABBANA; Chanel
Rouge Allure in Incandescente from
CHANEL. The Reform table is by FRISO
KRAMER at Van der Meerwich & Weston.

94

95

5.

How do you keep the magazine evolving?

If an outsider came to the first editorial meeting after an issue is back from the printers, they'd think none of us liked the magazine – 'That was a disaster, this didn't work …' – but it's just that we're Scottish and German and Dutch and that's how candid and fanatical it is in here. Everyone's completely focused on making sure each issue's better than the last. That said, I've found at other places I've worked that you've got to learn to make space for pleasure and joy as well as for critique and perfectionism, otherwise it can be a bit destructive.

What's the relationship of the magazine with the fashion industry? You are challenging the conventions and expectations about fashion media, but the industry has loved it and embraced it.

We started the magazine as an alternative to the women's fashion magazines out there, but speaking from inside the industry; we weren't trying to bite the hand that feeds us, because we love fashion. It's possible to present an intelligent view on fashion if it's done with high standards and reflects an appreciation of why most people are fascinated with fashion in the first place.

Do you think it's been a bit of a revelation to the industry?

Well, I would be rather grand if I sat here and told you that it has! I can see it's had some influence – of course we're heavily copied. We've coincided with a general shift in print publishing as a reaction to the Internet, and some aspects of that have been to our benefit, to the extent that it might seem as though we're leading the new phase. But I think it's fair to say that we've set a new standard for some elements of the industry, and that's great.

Léa

the gentlewoman

profile

Not many French actresses manage to cross the Euro-Hollywood divide. So how has Léa Seydoux, 28, succeeded so spectacularly where others have failed? Playing a blue-haired lesbian in the film that won this year's Palme d'Or at Cannes has only brought more offers from Los Angeles to her 10th-arrondissement apartment. Her allure lies in a combination of eloquence, intelligence and a killer pout. Her acting skills are instinctive – hereditary perhaps.

If Seydoux was British, we'd say she was posh (her family tree reads like a Who's Who of France's most prominent names). But she's French, so anything from *super douée* to *très tendance* will do.

Text by Horacio Silva
Portraits by Zoë Ghertner, styling by Anastasia Barbieri

196

6.

7. 8. 9.

The magazine has grown in pagination. Is that down to success with advertising revenue?

We've got just over 25 per cent advertising, which is an ideal balance for us. Plus, we've become heavier and we're using heavy, expensive paper. But yes, we've really grown – when you look at issue 1 now, it looks like a pamphlet.

How many do you print?

It's 89,000 copies at the moment. We started at 72,000, which was the same as *Fantastic Man* was printing at the time. That's at about 85,000 now; we're slightly more than that, but then the women's market is much bigger [than the men's]. So yes, it's grown in a shrinking market. We can't complain. There was a big increase in circulation with Angela and Adele in particular.

What are the key things for an aspiring magazine to get right for a launch issue?

You just need a really good idea that's very clearly expressed. Not everybody is going to see that issue, but if you get it right, it will act as a kind of mission statement for your readers and your team.

What advice would you give about starting a magazine?

Really, you just need to know [your idea] is right. If I could borrow somebody else's advice: I remember my friend [the curator] Charlotte Cotton telling me what her old boss at the V&A, Mark Haworth-Booth, once said to her: 'You've got to make your own contemporaries; you can't rely on the generation above you, the establishment, to throw you the crumbs from the table.' And I think that's right. The only way you can create something worth reading is if it's of your time and of your people.

6. *The Gentlewoman*, issue 8, Autumn/Winter 2013, Léa Sedoux photographed by Zoë Ghertner, styling by Anastasia Barbieri

7. *The Gentlewoman*, issue 5, Spring/Summer 2012, Christy Turlington photographed by Inez and Vinoodh

8. *The Gentlewoman*, issue 7, Spring/Summer 2013, Beyoncé photographed by Alasdair McLellan

9. *The Gentlewoman*, issue 9, Spring/Summer 2014, Vivienne Westwood photographed by Alasdair McLellan

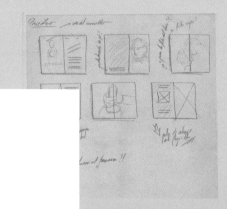

The anatomy of a magazine

Plan your title from cover styles to captions

Editorial structure and flat plans

Find your voice and vision

Essential magazine components

This is the fun part – giving shape to your vision and voice.

It's why you're in this game, and it's the antidote to all those headaches about distribution and cash flow.

A strong editorial voice and a clear vision are as important to the survival of your magazine as a considered publishing strategy. This comes straight from you, the maker. Your magazine is a paper and ink embodiment of your interests, ideals and passions. As the founder of *Disegno*, Johanna Agerman Ross, says, 'everything in *Disegno* is something I can stand and shout about from the rooftops.'

Confidence in your vision might sometimes mean sticking to your gut feeling even when the odds are against you, but readers will recognize and respond to something that comes from the heart. 'When I first launched *Anorak*,' says Cathy Olmedillas, 'everyone said "that's not going to work" – distributors, advertisers, everyone – because [the magazine] was unisex, the colour palette was too sophisticated, there was no character attached, no regular content … I think because *Anorak* is full of this warm passion … it's not a perfect product, it's not super-slick, it's obviously made out of passion, [and] I think the people who love it love it for the same reason, which is magical to me.'

Cereal magazine has a very clearly defined, unflinching visual style that is applied across every platform and detail, from the magazine itself to branding on product collaborations to its Pinterest board. 'A lot of stuff ends up on the cutting-room floor,' says its publisher, Rosa Park, of the process of paring back. 'That's always sad … but you have to make the best product you can.'

Clarity comes from confidence, although it might take a few issues before you really find your magazine's 'voice'. The best thing about magazines is that, even if you're not happy with the way something worked in one issue, you always have the next one to try a new concept, or to approach a regular feature in a different way.

"Start with a clear vision and then decide how to share it with the world."

Sarah Keough, *Put a Egg on It*

1.

1. *Put a Egg on It*, issue 6, photograph by Benjy Russell

Obsessive compulsive: personal passions

Gratuitous Type

Frequency: About once a year
Date launched: 2011
Location: New York City
Print run: 1,000–2,000
Strapline: 'A pamphlet of typographic smut'

From the 'always different' school of magazine design, Elana Schlenker's *Gratuitous Type* is an unabashed piece of graphic design and typographic 'porn'. It is a part-time pursuit for Schlenker, who is an independent designer, and it has been a tool for bringing new clients to her studio. 'I want readers to be as excited and inspired by the object as they are by the work it features,' she says. 'So the magazine follows the same size and format, but otherwise is redesigned for every issue, and each features its own unique production details.' She had fun with the title, which plays on the idea 'that you can put a big fat letter blown up on a page and designers [will] just drool over that. The intention was to set a light-hearted tone that was also self-aware, to acknowledge that the magazine is full of design and typography just for the sake of it.'

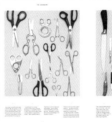

The Gourmand

Frequency: Biannual
Date launched: 2011
Location: London
Print run: 10,000
Strapline: 'A food and culture journal'

Food publishing has been revolutionized by the independent magazine scene, and sitting at the top table is *The Gourmand,* which was launched in June 2012. Eschewing reams of recipes, *The Gourmand* explores food's cultural and social significance as well as using it as a jumping-off point for visual creativity. 'We don't generally work with food specialists, but instead ask writers, photographers, set designers, art directors and illustrators working in other fields to produce work inspired by the subject,' says the magazine's editor-in-chief and creative director, David Lane. 'We are great believers that the content is king; the design is simply there to best communicate the message.'

Editorial structure

There are some editorial conventions and traditions that make a magazine a magazine, but when you're independent, the rules are there to be broken. Some magazines are completely different from issue to issue (*Mono.kultur*, *Gratuitous Type*), but to carry that off you need a watertight and enduring concept that justifies such an approach. Generally speaking, readers need some recognizable structure and familiar furniture by which to navigate your content. 'Don't make it too hard for your readers,' says Rob Orchard of *Delayed Gratification*. 'Point sizes and page numbers matter.'

See case studies of *Mono.kultur* on page 62 and *Gratuitous Type* and page 52

See section on Furniture, pages 64–67

Flat plans and pagination

A flat plan is the grid or map of your magazine's editorial structure, on to which you flesh out the contents of each issue. Flat plans are idiosyncratic and come in all shapes and sizes, from a pencil sketch in a notebook, to a neat and tidy spreadsheet, to a big production that fills an entire wall in the office. They serve a variety of purposes, both as an editorial tool and as a guide for the printer to the different elements of your magazine. As well as what content goes where, you can include information about paper stock changes, inserts, tip-ins and short pages.

The flat plan helps you to nail down the pagination of your magazine. Your printer will advise you to conform to the standard of 16-page sections, which is most economical for printing. But you can also create variation by adding 4-page or 8-page sections. Breaks between sections allow you to switch to different paper stocks or inks. As well as specifying the number of interior pages (let's say four 16-page sections, leading to an 8-page section, giving you a total of 64 + 8 = 72), you need to specify the cover as '+4', which indicates the cover, inside front cover, inside back cover and outside back cover, which will probably be on a different, heavier paper stock.

See page 142 for more about specifying your print job

The above are often abbreviated as:
IFC: inside front cover
IBC: inside back cover
OBC: outside back cover

2.

3.

2. With a team all living in different cities, each issue of *Acid* is planned digitally, using Skype and file sharing

3. When John Holt is working on *LAW* he makes a flat plan by printing out a page grid and inserting finished layouts, giving him an overview of the visual rhythm of an issue

4. *The Outpost* produces a final flat plan using digital layout files and includes a specification for the printer

5. Befitting its dedication to craft, the *Oh Comely* team plans out an issue's contents using a custom-made pegboard and colour-coded paper

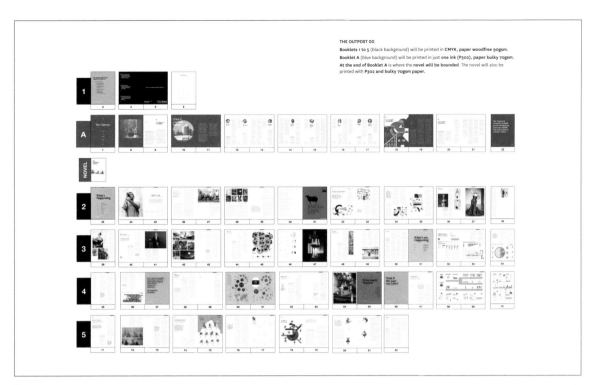

THE OUTPOST 00

Booklets 1 to 5 (black background) will be printed in **CMYK, paper woodfree 90gsm.**
Booklet A (blue background) will be printed in just **one ink (P302), paper bulky 70gsm.**
At the end of Booklet A is where the **novel will be bounded.** The novel will also be
printed with **P302 and bulky 70gsm paper.**

4.

5.

Sideways thinking and rule breaking

Wrap

Frequency: Biannual
Location: Oxford
Print run: 4,000–5,000
Magazine in three words: Brilliant
contemporary illustration
Size: 22 x 30 cm (8¾ x 11¾ in)

In making a magazine with a difference about the world of illustration, *Wrap*'s creators, Polly Glass and Chris Harrison, came up with a format that features interviews with illustrators but doubles as a practical product: the spreads can be removed and used as gift wrap. 'There's a perfect link to illustration by being paper-based,' they say, 'and a magazine is a relatively affordable item for customers to buy, allowing us to get as much exposure as possible for the contributing artists. Adding the wrapping-paper element gives *Wrap* a unique "usefulness" beyond being for reading, plus it's a fantastic way to show the illustrations on a bigger scale.'

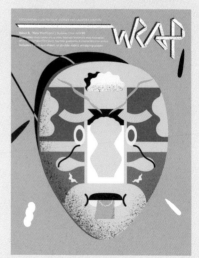

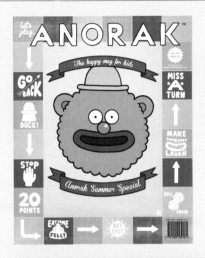

Anorak

Frequency: Five times per year
Location: London
Print run: 10,000
Cover price: £6
Number of pages: 64

In a sea of crassly produced, product-saturated children's magazines, *Anorak* is a genuine breath of fresh air. Its creator, Cathy Olmedillas, previously worked on the landmark 1990s style titles *Sleazenation* and *The Face*, a background that primed her to know what makes a magazine with a unique voice for a ready market. 'I became a mum, and that was the catalyst,' she recalls. 'I was amazed to see that there was no decent mag out there for children.' After publishing the magazine as a part-time venture for five years, she made some hard commercial decisions to take it to the next level as a self-sustaining business. By 2014 she was marking her eighth year with the 33rd edition of Anorak, a new iPad app and plans for two new titles.

6.

7.

8.

6. *Monocle*, issue 79,
December 2014–January 2015

7. *Cereal*, issue 6, 2013

8. *Noon*, issue 1, Spring/
Summer 2014

The cover

Perhaps the trickiest design challenge for a magazine to get right, the cover is often also the bit that is left until the last minute. The cover is a powerful visual ambassador on the shelf and can have a direct impact on sales. There is no magic formula; wildly different styles work brilliantly – just compare a densely populated *Monocle* cover with the sparse simplicity of a *Cereal* cover – but the most important job, and no mean feat, is to capture the spirit of the issue and your identity as a magazine.

See case study of *Riposte* on page 114

Riposte has been admired for its bold approach to cover design, turning the conventions of women's magazines on their head by relegating the 'cover photo' to the outside back page and putting a purely typographic design on the front. Danielle Pender, the magazine's founder and editor-in-chief, defines a great cover as 'something that perfectly and succinctly sums up the ethos of your magazine. Something that is bold and brave and doesn't follow trends.'

The fashion and art title *Noon* also commands respect for its cover style, where conventions are squarely kicked into the long grass: '*Noon* is a pretty niche title,' says its founder and editor-in-chief, Jasmine Raznahan, 'and that affords us a lot of liberty with regard to the cover. People might say I'm not the right person to ask what makes a great cover, because I put an older gentleman's naked bottom on the front of *Noon*'s first issue,' she quips, 'but I think the best covers are the bravest.'

Retailers and distributors report that a cover can be directly responsible for sales performance, for good and bad. 'Confusing covers that don't reflect the content don't work,' says Bryony Lloyd of the distributor Antenne Books. 'If you can sum up your magazine in one image, that's great. We've had issues where they haven't sold well purely based on the cover. Try and look at it with a fresh pair of eyes and get loads of feedback before you go to print,' she advises.

Liz Ann Bennett of *Oh Comely* magazine has a wonderful take on what makes a memorable magazine cover: 'It's like disembarking into a crowded train station and catching sight of a familiar face in the crowd,' she says. 'The challenge for magazine-makers is to create covers that fulfil both halves of this experience: attracting a reader's attention and coaxing [from them] a moment of recognition.'

More or less: cover type and image

Eye

Frequency: Quarterly
Date launched: 1990
Location: London
Cover price: £17
Strapline: 'The International Review of Graphic Design'

Eye is much admired for its beautiful design and high-quality production, and the cover is an important vehicle for its aesthetic values. Treated each time as an expanse of designable space, *Eye*'s cover is an object of beauty, shunning cover lines to concentrate on a single stunning image that represents the issue. 'The modern approach to an indie magazine', says *Eye*'s editor, John Walters, 'is: you get it out, find your audience. You might find your audience through a blog or website, or special-interest group. It's a bit like a band playing a few pubs and clubs and getting a following, and then using that as a sound basis for growing.'

PIN-UP

Frequency: Biannual
Date launched: October 2006
Location: New York City
Cover price: $25
Strapline: 'Magazine for Architectural Entertainment'

Just as carefully considered as *Eye*'s cover, but taking a completely different tack, the architectural title *PIN-UP* makes the typography of its cover lines the main event of the design. In an expression of the type-led design of the entire magazine, bold compositions of type on a photographic background advertise the content. This also reflects the magazine's editorial stance as 'a fun assembly of ideas, stories and conversations, paired with cutting-edge, specially commissioned photography and artwork'. Earlier issues even integrated the bar code into the ballet of type and images on the cover.

Shapeshifters: concept-driven design

Mono.kultur

Frequency: Quarterly
Location: Berlin
Print run: 7,000–10,000
Magazine in three words:
Quality, personality, integrity
Size: 15 x 20 cm (6 x 7¾ in)

A stalwart of the independent magazine world, *Mono.kultur* dishes up a surprise every issue, in terms of both content and design. Its concept is wonderfully simple: to present a long-form interview with a single artist, musician or creative person in each issue. The work and world of the interviewee inform the design concept and production, and the magazine's editor, Kai von Rabenau, works with a different designer each time. The only constant is its neat, small format; everything else in its production is open to interpretation. Highlights since its launch in 2005 have included tip-ins, posters, postcards and an issue with 12 encapsulated scents.

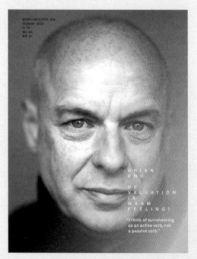

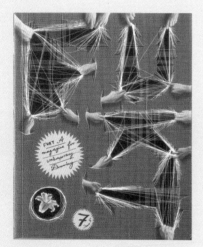

FUKT

Frequency: Annual
Date launched: 1999
Location: Berlin (since 2001; formerly Trondheim, Norway)
Print run: 3,000
Strapline: 'Contemporary Drawing'

FUKT magazine was something of a pioneer in the independent magazine world, launching as a self-funded, saddle-stitched title of 500 copies at the end of the 1990s. Its founder, the artist Björn Hegardt, runs the magazine as a non-profit adjunct to his creative practice. Today, each issue of *FUKT* is a splendiferous bespoke production. Hegardt and his team of contributors are on a mission 'to create the most beautiful and intriguing magazine we ever have seen', and so each edition is a surprise mix of production methods and design styles. The title is a play on the magazine's subject matter: 'Fukt means "moist" in Norwegian,' explains Hegardt, 'which somehow is the opposite to the dry paper and pen used for drawing. We liked the word, and also the English "meaning" of it.'

Editorial tone and style

The tone of voice of your written content creates the magazine's personality. Readers of *Smash Hits* in the 1980s will remember the funny interjections in brackets throughout the articles from 'the Ed'. Develop a style for the way you write things like titles, standfirsts and captions: they will become familiar friends. *The Gentlewoman* is known for its witty captions and also uses formulae, such as first names instead of the more formal 'Mr' prefixes of its male counterpart *Fantastic Man*, 'like women talking to each other; a warmth in the tone of voice', says the magazine's art director, Veronica Ditting.

Marc Robbemond of the magazine retailer Athenaeum in Amsterdam is perfectly placed to observe the character traits of the magazines that 'make it', since he handles thousands of titles a year. 'By being super-distinctive and choosing a topic that you know you will find interesting over a long period,' he says, 'those are the [qualities of] magazines that are succeeding. For example, *The Outpost* ... has a strong concept – there is going to be a lot to write about the Middle East and the possibilities for the Middle East in the coming years.'

"From the biggest idea to the smallest detail, everything is very considered, it's done in The Gentlewoman 'way'."

Veronica Ditting, *The Gentlewoman*

9.

9. *The Gentlewoman*, issue 6, Autumn/Winter 2014, 'Terribly nice jumpers with Yasmin Le Bon', photography by Alasdair McLellan, styling by Jonathan Kaye

Furniture

From page numbers to ISSNs, some elements of a magazine's 'furniture' are standard, some are optional, and others are pretty essential. Every magazine approaches these elements in a different way, but it helps your readers if you have a consistent and considered approach. The way you handle them can also subtly set the tone of your magazine. Here's a handy checklist of elements and terminology:

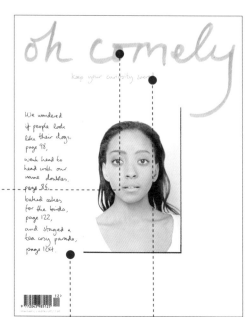

10.

Title/masthead/logo

The magazine's title, sometimes called the masthead, acts as a logo, but sometimes magazines also have an icon or monograph (see *Monocle*'s 'M' and *Esquire*'s 'Esky').

Coverlines

Decide if these teasers about the issue's contents will be part of your cover strategy. This is more important if your magazine depends on news-stand sales.

11.

Strapline

Sum up your magazine in ten words or fewer.

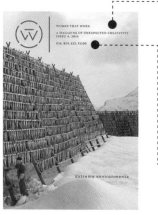

12.

Price

Include the price in your native currency and, if you have fixed prices in other regions, include those too. They must be fixed with your distributor.

13.

Issue number/date

Emphasize collectibility, and think about how several issues will look lined up on the bookshelf.

14.

ISSN

Any 'serial' publication needs an International Standard Serial Number (ISSN), a unique number that identifies the publication and forms part of the bar code. Read more about the system and find out where to request an ISSN in your country on the ISSN International Centre's website: issn.org/. Apply in good time: allow a month to get your ISSN.

Bar code

All publications that charge a cover price need a bar code, which will be scanned at the point of sale in shops. You need a new bar code for each issue of your magazine. Once you have your ISSN (see left), you can buy bar code images online from several websites, including buyabarcode.co.uk in the UK and buyabarcode.com in the US. They typically cost about £15 each, with discounts for buying in bulk. Retailers will enter your bar code number into their system; when it is scanned at the till, it will bring up the issue information and price. Distributors and retailers like bar codes to be displayed clearly on front covers, but magazine designers often look for a way to avoid having unsightly bar codes interrupting their covers. A detailed document about bar coding is available from the Professional Publishers Association, ppa.co.uk.

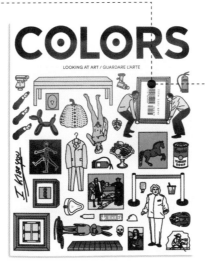

10. *Oh Comely*, issue 12, photo Agatha A. Nitecka, model Michelene Auguste at Models 1

11. *The Forecast* (*Monocle*'s annual publication), issue 1, 2015

12. *Works That Work*, issue 4, 2014, photograph by George F Mobley/National Geographic/Getty

13. *The White Review*, issues 6–10

14. *Delayed Gratification*, issue 12, January–March 2012

15. *Colors*, issue 87, 'Looking at Art'

15.

Inside:

16.

Contributors' page

A place to profile the writers, photographers and illustrators whose work has gone into this particular issue. Nosy readers will enjoy a photo of the person. Some magazines have fun with the way they profile people, such as asking everyone a particular question related to the theme of the issue.

17.

Book

The meat in the sandwich, the central section where readers will find long-form features, interviews, profiles and photostories.

Special report

This will be relevant if you explore a special topic in each issue, with a collection of articles exploring the theme from different angles.

19.

Back section

Usually the place for more short- to mid-length regular reads, such as reviews, opinion columns and short features.

18.

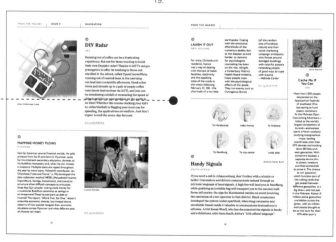

20.

Front section

Most magazines use the front section for regular bite-sized and short-read pieces, such as news, product profiles, letters, event guides, short profiles and opinion columns.

21.

Credits

Don't forget to give proper credit to illustrators and photographers for every image – including the cover.

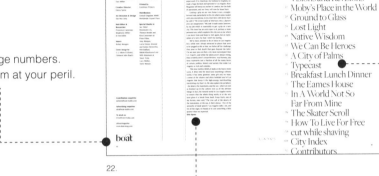

22.

Folios

Also known as page numbers. Dispense with them at your peril.

Editor's letter

A personal note from the editor to the reader, this sets the editorial tone, discusses the issue's theme and points to highlights to be found throughout the issue.

Contents

A list of the magazine's sections and articles, with page references.

Masthead/colophon

Names and contact details of the editorial staff and other key people (such as your advertising sales contact), publishing information (including the publisher's name, the frequency of the magazine), postal and website address, subscription information, print and paper information (are your suppliers FSC, Forest Stewardship Council, certified, for example?).

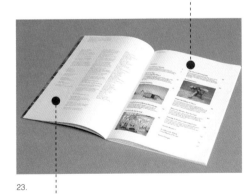

23.

16. *Weapons of Reason*, issue 1, 2014

17. *Weapons of Reason*, issue 1, 2014, photography by Cristian Barnett

18. *Riposte*, issue 4, 2015, featuring cover of *The Face* by Elaine Constantine, 1999

19. *Makeshift*, issue 9, 'Navigation' special report, photography by Karolle Rabarison

20. *Makeshift*, issue 9, 'From The Makery' front section

21. *Anorak*, issue 32, 'Spot the Difference' double-page spread, illustrated by Harry Sankey

22. *Boat*, issue 8, 2014, Los Angeles

23. *Works that Work*, issue 1, Winter 2013

Within articles:

Title

Setting parameters for the way you title articles will give personality to your tone of voice.

24.

26.

25.

Standfirst

A short paragraph that introduces the topic and tempts people to read on. Resist the lazy option of simply using the first paragraph of the author's text here.

Pull quotes

Juicy quotations from the text pulled out and stylishly presented; they're a way to draw the reader on through longer texts, and provide an extra visual component to layouts.

Box-outs

Extra background information on an article's topic, presented in easily digested form alongside the main copy.

Captions

Every image needs a caption. Even if it seems obvious to you what an image is, the reader expects to have a quick reference point whether they're flicking through or reading in a concentrated fashion. There's room to be playful with your copy here. Make sure you use a clear, logical numbering system.

27.

24. *Riposte*, issue 4, 2015, 'Life Lessons' feature, illustration by Rebecca Clarke

25. *Works That Work*, issue 2, 2013, photography by Bonjwing Lee

26. *Delayed Gratification*, issue 14, January–March 2014

27. *The Gentlewoman*, issue 8, Autumn/Winter 2013

Brave new world: Middle East mags

The Carton

Frequency: Biannual (formerly quarterly)
Date launched: July 2011
Location: Beirut, Lebanon
Strapline: 'A magazine about food, culture and the Middle East'

'When we first started, in 2010–11, independent magazine publishing in the Middle East was close to non-existent,' says *The Carton*'s editor and art director, Jade George, 'and the concept of "food culture" was not understood in the region.' Along with a few other pioneering titles, *The Carton* champions the fast-evolving cultural life of the region, leading the way in galvanizing a new generation of thinkers, writers, artists and designers. Aside from the magazine, George and her co-founder, Rawan Gebran, run the micro-publishing house Art and Then Some and the Love Print collective.

The Outpost

Frequency: Biannual (formerly quarterly)
Date launched: September 2012
Location: Beirut, Lebanon
Strapline: 'A magazine of possibilities'

Born out of the Arab Spring, *The Outpost* occupies a position at the forefront of a new publishing community. 'My team and I wanted to create a media outlet to help us better understand the place we live in and make sense of it,' says its founder, Ibrahim Nehme, '[and] to help us challenge and break stereotypes and shift perspectives. We wanted *The Outpost* to have an archival role in documenting how the Arab world is changing, how we as Arab youth are helping to change it, and how we are also changing with it, especially during this transformative historic period.' Both *The Outpost* and *The Carton* are members of the Love Print collective (along with *WTD Magazine* and *The State*), which unites indie magazines in the Middle East and pools experience, resources and buying power.

1.

Interview
The Editor &
Art Director

John Walters &
Simon Esterson,
Editor & Art Director
Eye

This formidable and much-respected duo in the magazine-publishing world share many years' experience, on *Eye* magazine and many other titles. *Eye* is their baby, following a management buyout from its previous owner, Haymarket, in 2008. Walters and Esterson now own the title and run it from a studio in Hoxton, east London. Here they reveal what was entailed in the shift from corporate ownership to independence, and share their wisdom on the world of indie magazines.

What's happening in the independent magazine landscape at the moment? Which magazines are shaping it?

JW: Many people are using new business models, things like Kickstarter and Unbound, ways of financing the magazine before it's printed. That can make magazines with quite short print runs work.

2.

SE: Things are completely open about the content, the business model and the way you want to publish, so you can make something you're comfortable with and reduce those big, fixed risks that go with publishing. It's not necessarily true that you'll make any money … For lots of people who make independent magazines, making money is not the primary requirement. Covering your costs is usually a requirement, but people are doing it for other reasons, too. That's why those magazines are exciting.

There was a period when you picked up lots of mainstream magazines in newsagents and they were all a bit 'me too', a bit derivative, nothing terribly exciting. Now, if you go to a Printout event [run in London by Steven Watson of subscription service Stack and Jeremy Leslie of MagCulture blog] or a Facing Pages conference [biennial event in The Netherlands] or read Jeremy Leslie's blog, there are a lot of people who are simply passionate about saying something or showing something, and that usually makes quite an interesting magazine.

What does being independent mean for you in the way you make a magazine?

SE: The wonderful thing about independent magazines is that you have all these options about how you want to make a magazine. You can decide whether you want to sell advertising. You can try to distribute through bookshops, or you can try to distribute by selling single copies on the Internet. You can put those modules together to make the kind of magazine you want, that you feel comfortable with.

Almost by definition, independence means a small, agile team – looking after subscriptions and promotions, liaising with the advertising sales people and making sure we order enough mailing boxes for the next issue. Those jobs all get done between John and me at some point.

JW: Not forgetting social media strategy. Some magazines have a whole department for that.

1. John Walters (left) and Simon Esterson (right), photograph by Ivan Jones

2. *Eye*, issue 80, Summer 2011, image by Field for GF Smith

SE: That all seems like a lot of work, which it is, but also it's very easy because we just talk about it every day and we don't have to go to meetings where we have to explain to somebody who is looking after ten magazines … we just get on with it.

JW: Indie magazines are in a really interesting phase. It's a little difficult to see where it might go, because you can't keep running a magazine purely on love and enthusiasm for that long, unless it turns into something else.

SE: I think you can, but you have to be realistic about your expectations and your willingness to put in the time. What you're investing is time.

JW: Yes, it's time and also the enthusiasm of the readership, which changes over time, too … Some magazines flare up and catch a moment in culture, and their time might pass, but other magazines might do that and then become part of the firmament. Take a magazine like *MixMag*, which was of the moment and has survived. *The Word* [published 2003–12], which Mark Ellen edited, was very of its moment, but didn't have a long life as a magazine.

3.

3. *Eye*, issue 87, Spring 2014, photograph by Lee Funnell

4. *Eye*, issue 80, Summer 2011, article on 20 years of graphic design, image by Alvin Lustig

5. *Eye*, issue 81, Autumn 2011, image detail by Helmo and John McConnell

Can you identify a recipe for longevity? What has enabled *Eye* to keep going from issue to issue?

JW: With a magazine going back to 1990, and running a website in parallel, I'm certainly very conscious of the legacy of *Eye* and the fact that it's still valued a great deal. So in a way we're using the past archive to communicate that we're in this for the long term, and that we're going to carry on. Being a quarterly, you can never be right up to the minute, you can never be trendy in the way that a monthly or weekly can, so you have to take a longer view. Having said that, sometimes we'll 'luck into' things where we catch the moment.

SE: Our advantage is all those things, but also that it's a niche. If you're close to your niche and talk to a lot of people, inevitably you stumble on things. You know about things and hear about things, and that's exciting. You're not sitting in an office responding to press releases.

JW: When you look at the mainstream magazine industry, there is an unholy alliance between advertisers, PR companies and editorial teams, who are all working in the same area. When you are much more independent you can just follow certain interests and obsessions. As Simon says, we're very immersed in the culture of graphic design so we know about stuff, sometimes without even knowing we know. Our writers are doing the same and coming to us with their reflections. With *Eye*, we aim to do pieces that aspire to some of the qualities of a book, without actually being a book.

20

YEARS OF CHANGE **GRAPHIC DESIGN IN PAST PRESENT & FUTURE DECADES**

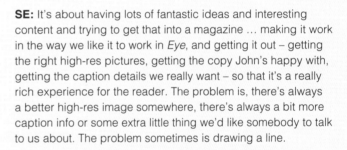

DREAMS CAN COME TRUE

As previously opposing worlds collide, Johnny Hardstaff envisages new designer-client relationships

CRASHING AND BURNING

Design and business make a volatile mix, says Jim Northover, but it is one we cannot afford to dismiss

4.

SE: It's about having lots of fantastic ideas and interesting content and trying to get that into a magazine … making it work in the way we like it to work in *Eye*, and getting it out – getting the right high-res pictures, getting the copy John's happy with, getting the caption details we really want – so that it's a really rich experience for the reader. The problem is, there's always a better high-res image somewhere, there's always a bit more caption info or some extra little thing we'd like somebody to talk to us about. The problem sometimes is drawing a line.

JW: Yes, it's [a case of] what level of obsessive detail are we prepared to forgo?

You have to go to print at some point and then there'll always be another issue, which you're probably already thinking about. That's the essence of the magazine medium, isn't it?

JW: The medium of the magazine is, I find, a fantastically satisfying way of presenting quite disparate visual material, styles and forms of writing. Obviously within a certain culture of publishing you establish that you can treat some things quite lightly and go into incredible depth on other things. If you have that relationship with your readers, which I think we're fortunate to have, you can present that and they feel they get something very satisfying. And it's something you can go back to, whether online or by keeping it on your shelves and still getting something out of it. Simon is an incredibly experienced

5.

6.

7.

magazine designer doing a lot of other magazines in parallel with *Eye*, so we are the beneficiaries of [long experience] in the mainstream … there are many skills and core values that we bring to an indie magazine that [mean it's much easier than] if you were starting off the streets.

SE: But some of those things make us boring old farts. We like a mag that we would describe as 'properly subbed', but I read magazines that aren't properly subbed and, if it's a great magazine, I'm not that bothered. I'm more interested in the energy that comes off it. I think you recognize that energy … My favourite current magazine is this little risograph-printed Australian bike magazine called *Head Full of Snakes*. It's just brilliant content, [and] the form is absolutely perfect.

See page 99 to read more about *Head Full of Snakes*

JW: There's an interesting thing happening within the DIY magazine world … Before I became a journalist I was a musician, and in the music 'zine world of the late 1970s and '80s, you could have a roughly produced magazine – full of mistakes, not properly subbed, terrible pictures – but if it had energy it would do its job, particularly in music, where people don't care about pictures so much as in fashion or photography. You would get little 'zines where the form expressed the instant nature of what was being produced.

The original *i-D* magazine [launched by Terry Jones in 1980] is an interesting case because Terry Jones, an incredibly experienced art director, just went back to the kitchen table and stapled together A4 sheets. There you see a real art director's confidence and editorial vision, and a bunch of writers all obsessed with their subject.

If you were doing something like that now, you would try to make it look a lot more professional, and it would be a lot better bound and printed, but it might still be a bit tatty in terms of the way it was written and edited and so on. And that can produce a weird kind of mismatch. I'm not saying this either as a problem or as a solution, but from time to time I come across what looks like a really exciting film magazine, say, and they've got great high-res pictures and great illustration, and then you start to read it and you think, 'Hm, I'd like to read [articles by] someone who actually knows what they're talking about.' We're in an interesting state of flux.

What about the way the Internet has become a tool for publishers?
SE: It's about a relationship with the audience. Clearly, if you've got a blog that works, why not make a magazine or book or something for that same audience? Online is a fantastic way of keeping in touch with everybody and selling subscriptions and single copies. The world of bookshops and newsagents is under pressure. Putting a £17 magazine in a general newsagent was always difficult, but it's become very difficult now.

For me, the biggest, most interesting thing about the rise of online [publishing] has been its relationship with magazine cycles. It's very difficult to publish a good weekly now. You have to do something very, very special or you'll just be a responsive website. Monthly gets interesting: you've got to have some kind of content that people don't just want to absorb online, perhaps a certain kind of information or really smart analysis. *The Economist* will probably survive as a weekly because of its smart analysis and very good summary. Then, when you start getting into quarterlies, you are outside that news and events cycle and using your instincts about what readers are interested in.

8.

What's the distribution model for *Eye*?
SE: It is about 50–60 per cent subscriber. Then it's worldwide news-stand, which can be anything from a shop like Tate Modern bookshop [in London] to a little newsagent that takes a few copies.

The big distribution houses are interested in the indie magazines that are going to 'make it'. They're interested in volume, because they make money from high-volume sales. So a big distribution house will be interested in *Fantastic Man* and *The Gentlewoman* and *Monocle*, and won't be interested in something selling 1,000 copies inside the M25. It's just not worth it for them, since the profits aren't enough for the time they'll have to spend on it.

Despite the distribution challenges, is independent publishing having 'a moment'?
JW: Look at all the events and conferences: Facing Pages, the Printout events, the Magpile Awards. There are a lot of people who want to make a magazine from a personal obsession, and people already working in publishing who really want to do their own thing.

6. *Eye*, issue 83, Spring 2012, image detail by Massimo Vignelli

7. *Eye*, issue 88, Summer 2014, photo by George Hurrell

8. *Eye*, issue 85, Spring 2013, profile of Chris Dixon, image by Platon

SE: It would be wrong to think that this is the only moment there's ever been for independent publishing. There have been various interesting moments in the past when a tectonic shift has enabled people to do things in a different way. But today it's wide open: there's always a better flat plan, a better picture, a better way of organizing things. You can put any amount of energy into it, because there's no wrong or right.

Ink and pixels

Mapping your media

Strategies for how print, online and social platforms can work together

The idea that print is 'dead' is surely dead itself.

The boom in the independent magazine world has proved that there is an appetite for well-made printed publications. A lot has been said about the Internet being a disaster for publishing, and indeed it has made fast-paced news in print increasingly redundant, but for independent magazines it is an important ally. Indies tend to publish between one and four times a year, so the speed of digital publishing is not a threat. Indie titles make the most of what it means to be in print – long-form journalism, wonderful layouts, good design and high-quality production and papers. The Internet is an essential tool for independent magazine businesses to spread the word, talk more frequently to their community and maintain a shopfront.

'We started out just the two of us in our mid-twenties and we didn't really know anyone,' says Benjamin Eastham, co-founder of print quarterly *The White Review*. 'The Internet allowed us to reach people really quickly. We were able to attract a readership early, [and] reach people through Twitter and Facebook … Having a website allows us to keep bringing people back between issues. It's brand recognition, and we have ten times the readership online. We've always embraced it.'

Print's charming

Printed layouts are all about hierarchy and editorial choices. Your authority as the person or team electing what to talk about, photograph and illustrate should shine through, and that editing of stories and information creates the character that readers want to buy into. It's the antidote to the relentless onslaught of content online, and is often the special ingredient that makes indie titles stand out from the commercial titles on the newsagent's shelf.

Print is tangible. When people part with cash for a magazine, it's because they want to feel it in their hands. The quality of the paper and the printing, the weight and shape, the way the binding opens, the flick and fall of the pages – all these things are part of a magazine's character, and transform a bookshop browser into a committed buyer.

Whether your production budget extends to toothsome features or is more modest, you can hold your reader's attention for longer in print. While online habits are suited to 'snacking' and hopping from link to link, in print long-form writing and plenty of space for amazing photography and illustration come into their own. Print is a medium for contemplation that people collect and return to.

1.

1. *The White Review*, issues 6–10

2.

3.

Rob Orchard says that celebrating the special qualities of print was one of the motivations for him and his team when they set up *Delayed Gratification* and initiated the 'slow journalism' movement. But an online medium still has a role: 'While we love print magazines and worry about the impact digital is having on journalism,' he says, 'the Internet is essential for research and for spreading the word about our project, and is the principal medium through which we sell subscriptions.'

One of Kai Brach's motivations for starting the print magazine *Offscreen*, which tells the stories of digital creators, was, he says, a growing sense of unease about the fragility of digital creations. He had spent thousands of hours being creative online, but it amounted to information that could be deleted totally in a second. 'I rediscovered "the edges of print",' says the web designer-turned-publisher, 'the joy of entering and exiting a text and closing a book when you finish. It was away from the Internet of hyper-connectivity, where you never meet the edge.'

This is echoed by Eastham of *The White Review*: 'I felt very strongly that for a mag to survive as a physical object it has to take advantage of the format, be beautifully designed and be on good paper,' he says, 'to be an object that people want to collect in a similar way to how people want to collect works of art.'

2. *Delayed Gratification* pioneered the 'slow journalism' movement

3. *Offscreen* looks at the universe of digital media via a printed format

Print

★ A special object to collect and keep
★ Has longevity on the retail shelf and on the bookshelf at home
★ Holds the reader's attention with long-form articles
★ Offers space for creative layouts and use of photography and illustration
★ Impact in the retail environment
★ High-end print appeals to advertisers

Production takes centre stage

The White Review

Frequency: Quarterly
Date launched: February 2011
Print run: 1,500
Cover price: £12.99
Number of pages: 172

The makers of *The White Review* have a background in art books, and these production values shine through in their magazine. 'If we were going to bother going to the expense of producing a magazine, we were going to invest a lot of time, energy and initial start-up costs in making a beautiful object that was collectible and gave people a reason to buy it,' says its editor, Benjamin Eastham. More than justifying itself as a printed object of value and collectibility, *The White Review* features production feats like a folded poster dust jacket, a contents page on a booklet insert, stock changes, extra bound-in sections, inserted postcards and tip-ins.

IdN

Frequency: Bi-monthly
Date launched: 1992
Print run: 50,000–90,000
Cover price: $19.95
Number of pages: 108

Born out of the digital advances in design and production of the 1980s and '90s, Hong Kong-based *IdN* ('international designers' network') has survived and evolved through galloping developments in those fields. It presents an interesting mix of digital content in a printed format, often exploring adventurous print and production techniques. '*IdN* began as an experiment in digital publishing,' says its director, Chris Ng. 'One of the catalysts was when Laurence [Ng, *IdN*'s founder and publisher] chatted to John Warnock, co-founder of Adobe Systems, at the time when the three visionaries (Warnock, Steve Jobs of Apple Computers and Paul Brainerd of Aldus) teamed up to build the first LaserWriter [1985].' The LaserWriter was at the forefront of the desktop publishing revolution in the 1980s, paving the way for a new era of indie publishers.

Digital love

Anyone embarking on a publishing project today has to consider a digital offering alongside their print-and-paper incarnation. At the very least, your website is a place to sell copies direct to readers – the most financially efficient route to copy-sales revenue because you're not giving a percentage of the cover price to a middleman. When you're planning your model and allocating time, money and resources, do not forget about digital – even if your heart is well and truly devoted to print.

'If you want to be a commercial player,' says *Dazed & Confused* publisher Jefferson Hack, 'being print-only will keep you out of part of the conversation. I'm not saying it has to be a bells-and-whistles dot-com, but you need to have a digital strategy for what you're doing.'

'Print is the most important, in that it's the thing I'm most passionate about,' says Rosa Park of *Cereal*. 'But print and digital are equally important for the business. They're very different and they do different things for us. Digital allows amazing instant, constant interaction with our readership.'

Monocle uses its digital content as an incentive for subscribers, with exclusive content that is accessible only with a subscription to the print magazine. *Makeshift* magazine offers discounts on the price of subscriptions for individuals in exchange for 'shares' on its social-media platforms.

While you should not lose sight of your core product – the printed magazine – digital platforms allow you to do many things that are not possible in print, such as video content and quick-release editorial. Recognizing and playing to the strengths of each medium is key. Make the most of the Internet's unique capabilities by creating bespoke content not seen in the magazine, and even charge for it or offer it as a subscriber's perk.

Your website can also help you to generate advertising revenue. If you're talking to brands about space in your magazine, you can also offer them a package that includes online space. It's a bargaining chip, and might bump your revenue by precious hundreds or even thousands of pounds.

4.

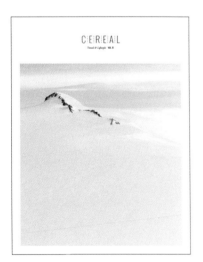

5.

Digital

★ Attracts a high volume of readers
★ Direct online sales of magazine copies have high profit margins
★ Great for promoting new issues, events and products
★ Creates additional traction with advertisers
★ Offers a fast and ongoing interaction with readership

Social media

Social media is a powerful tool for independent publishers. Even with no marketing budget, an independent title can promote sales with a strong social-media base. Social media is your biggest friend when it comes to building up an online community, and that is important if you are trying to drive sales through your website and let people know when your latest issue is in the shops.

'As the [print] magazine is published quite infrequently,' says Luke Wood of *Head Full of Snakes*, 'people keep up with where we're at through the blog and Twitter. One of the key moments for us was the first issue being written about on Pipeburn (a big custom motorcycle blog) and MagCulture. That kind of engagement online … has been vital to the success of the magazine.'

Read an interview with Tyler Brûlé on pages 122–27

Wield the power of social media with care: have a plan. Tyler Brûlé, publisher of *Monocle*, is in the fortunate position of not needing to rely on social media at all, but his thoughts on how it can dilute the power or integrity of a magazine brand are interesting. Think about how you want to present your title on social media. Consider the benefits of giving people an intimate insight into your world versus the risk of jeopardizing the mystique that draws readers to your title.

'We would never put anything on social media that we wouldn't put in the magazine,' says Rosa Park of *Cereal*. 'Whether you're reading our magazine, reading a blog post, looking at our Instagram or flicking through Tumblr, any of those channels on their own should give you a very clear indication of who we are and what we do. That's our approach to social media, rather than "Hey, here's a snap of our office today."'

6.

7.

4. *Cereal*'s website has a shop selling product collaborations between the magazine and carefully chosen brand partners

5. *Cereal*, issue 8, 2014

6. *Offscreen* maker Kai Brach actively interacts with readers via social media between issues of his quarterly print title. Photograph by June Kim

7. Magazines like *Makeshift* perfect the use of mobile platforms to put their content in reader's pockets daily

Social media

★ Creates instant engagement and allows for conversation with readers
★ High-volume reach
★ Useful for promoting sales and readership by directing traffic to other online platforms

A leap of faith: digital to print

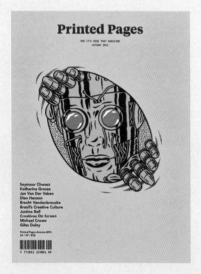

Printed Pages

Frequency: Quarterly
Date launched: March 2013
Cover price: £5
Strapline: 'A quarterly magazine focusing on depth and discovery across the art and design world'

Part of a growing trend for blogs that become print magazines, *Printed Pages* is the second incarnation of the magazine produced by INT Works (formerly It's Nice That), the graphic design studio of Will Hudson and Alex Bec. The first was the eponymous *It's Nice That*, launched in 2009 off the back of the popular graphic design blog. 'We had the benefit that we had built up an audience online,' says Hudson. 'When we launched the first issue we had just hit 100,000 uniques [visitors] to the site each month. We printed 1,500 copies and sold out in four or five weeks.' After shelving the model for *It's Nice That* (see page 28) they relaunched in 2013 as *Printed Pages*.

Sidetracked

Frequency: Triannual
Date launched: April 2014
Cover price: £10
Strapline: 'Adventure Inspired'

The graphic designer John Somerton began his magazine as a web project in 2011 when he quite literally got sidetracked by his love of adventure pursuits. He launched a print version in 2014 because 'print is in my blood', as he says. 'The website had grown to a point that it had become a respected and valued source of adventure-related content … So, with the recent resurgence of independent print, I thought it was time to give it a go. The reaction was incredible! I love print – holding a physical copy, flicking through the smooth, uncoated stock, and even the smell of the inks, is a special feeling, and one that just can't be replicated in the digital world.'

With 20 years' experience in the magazine trade, Sasha Simic of the London distribution company Central Books is brilliantly placed to advise on the process of getting your magazine to retailers. Central has a reputation for working with niche titles, and was set up in 1936 by the Communist Party to distribute left-wing literature. There is an echo of that in Central's willingness to take on progressive magazines, but today the company represents a broad spectrum of titles and retailers across the globe.

What type of magazine do you distribute?

We get two sorts of publisher coming to us. Firstly, professionals who have been doing it for a bit but who need bigger or different market penetration … And then – and this is the more fun side of the business – people who have put together a magazine and have no idea where to go from there. Or they've got a rough idea – they've tucked two or three copies under their arm and gone round to shops like Magma or Artwords [both in London] to say 'Will you take this magazine?' Sometimes retailers say 'Yes,' and will [stock it] for a bit. Sometimes they say: 'You need a distributor, you need to consolidate all that, there's a logistical problem to doing this one-to-one.'

1.

Interview
The Distributor

Sasha Simic
Central Books

What are the basic steps in the distribution service you offer?

We tell people to concentrate on putting the magazine together, and we concentrate on the problem of getting it to the market. We've got a fairly standard contract that pays publishers on the basis of sales, not on how many copies go into the market. It's done on a particular cycle. Essentially the contract breaks down to a 55/45 percentage of the cover price. We get 55 per cent. The first thing to say is that we don't keep all that; we share it with the retailers. We also take on things like shipping, so actually we end up with far less than 55 per cent.

My job, once we've agreed and swapped contracts, is to build a standing order for the magazine. There are three stages to how a publisher should approach its marketing process. The best way of selling a magazine is through subscription, because subscription means guaranteed sales. If somebody takes out a year's subscription, it's money in the bank. What a retailer relationship should be about is getting a magazine out there and getting people to buy it spontaneously. The idea is to turn that into a regular relationship, where [readers are] waiting for the next issue to come out, and ultimately become subscribers, [since a] subscriber represents a more steady income supply for a publisher.

To begin the process – let's say for an art magazine – I'll get on the phone and email, go and see people, and say 'We're taking on an art title.' I'll go to the Tates and Koenig Books, Magma [and so on] and build a core set of standing orders, which means that we can then talk to [publishers] regularly about what it means in terms of their print runs.

For many magazines we won't be the only outlet, although for some we are. By and large, we don't deal with the news trade; we start with bookshops, the chains and independents, and we go with art galleries and museums, because that's essentially what our portfolio is about.

Is it international?

Yes, we operate in the UK, Europe, the Far East – we have a portfolio of outlets in Singapore, Hong Kong, Taiwan, Japan, Australia and New Zealand. It could be a single shop, like Glee Books in Sydney, or people who are distributors in their own right, like Gordon & Gotch in New Zealand.

You're the broker between the publishers on one side and the retailers on the other, is that right?

Exactly, and I'm building up a set of standing orders that will help a publisher to fix its print run. Say a new magazine comes to us, and I manage to get standing orders for 800 copies: that would be the initial 'magazine release'. Big news-orientated firms like Menzies or WHSmith will do a release every day. We do one once a week. That means that when a new magazine comes in it's added to the list. I press a button on Thursdays and we produce hundreds of invoices for retail orders that get sent out.

If a retailer has a standing order to take five or ten copies, that doesn't restrict them; it doesn't mean that's all they're going to get. If they sell out, they just get on the phone and ask me to send another five.

1. Sasha Simic, portrait by Ivan Jones

What should people think about when planning distribution into their publishing model?

[The method of] sale or return affects what people are paid. So perhaps the biggest cheque you'll ever get from us as a publisher starting off with a new magazine is the first one. I get, say, 800 copies out to the market. If it's a quarterly [the publisher will] get a cheque that pretty much reflects that. The following cheque will be affected by the returns – the money varies according to how many copies are returned by the retailers. In the UK, retailers have up to three months to return a monthly title from invoice; they've got twice that for bi-monthlies, and nearly a year for quarterlies. So don't go and spend all of your first cheque.

2.

You see many magazines: can you recognize which will be successful? What's your selection process?

We get offered at least five or six new magazines a week. I turned on my computer this morning and there were three emails from publishers saying 'We'd like you to consider this title.' To begin the process, we ask people to send copies to us. Sometimes somebody sends us an email saying that they're thinking of putting a mag together and would like to meet us to discuss it. With no title and no actual magazine there's not an awful lot we can do. Today we often get PDFs. But we prefer to start with a concrete magazine if we can, even if it's just a mock-up – it gives you an idea of what it will look like.

Every month we sit down and go through magazines to discuss what we will take on. There are no set rules. For example, we don't have any sports mags in our portfolio, but when we got a magazine called *8x8* in, we saw that it was beautifully designed and I passed it on to people who know about football. They say it's wonderfully written and fits with what we do. That's the only thing that really guides us: does it fit with our portfolio? Does it fit with the ethos of the company?

What are the biggest no-nos for a magazine, from a distributor's perspective?

A common mistake by publishers is to think that a change of format will break the glass ceiling or constrictions in the market, and that people will be led to it. Actually, there's a reason why most magazines are roughly A4 – there are problems with stacking and displaying [those of different sizes]. Tinkering with the format and thinking that in itself will make a magazine more interesting and lead to sales is a turn-off for us.

The other thing is the look of the magazine. Presentation is important. It's got to look good, and there's no reason why it shouldn't in this day and age.

Thirty per cent of all printed material in the UK goes through WHSmith. Is it necessary for magazines to be distributed by them?

No. And just as well, because to be honest it's tough for a small publisher to get into WHSmith. Firstly, it controls what it puts out. Secondly, it can ask for discounts that any publisher that is just going by sales is not going to survive. The reason titles like

Cosmopolitan are in WHSmith is because they don't function on what they sell, they function on advertising, and they need to be in places like WHSmith [in order to] have the sales figures. But it's highly unlikely that WHSmith would take a small publisher on, and if it did it could ask terms that would make it very difficult. If you're starting up, I wouldn't think in terms of WHSmith. Places like us and Comag and Worldwide Magazine distribution in Birmingham are the sensible route to distribution. And good luck to you if you get big enough to deal with WHSmith.

How do you feel about the health of the magazine market today?
It's difficult. Part of that is what's been happening for the last ten years. I started at Central Books in 2000. Waterstones had a magazine department in most of its branches and took the kind of magazines that we distribute – literary and art titles. Some branches took them in really significant quantities: the shop on Long Acre in London took huge numbers of design and art titles. At that time, Borders had just started; in 2000 it had its Oxford Street shop and was opening Charing Cross. By 2005/6 it had about 50 branches.

Back then, my job was really easy. If someone came to us with a new title, I'd get on the phone to Borders' central buyer and recommend quantities for different shops, and immediately we had standing orders for significant quantities. That meant magazines got visibility. The sales weren't that strong, though. When Borders went out of the ring in 2009 we did some really hard number-crunching, which was very interesting. Borders' Oxford Street shop did phenomenally well, and the Charing Cross and Islington shops did really well too. Those three branches were responsible for 60 per cent of all its magazine sales. Beyond a few regional branches, its other shops didn't do well, but you got the illusion of visibility. It would take literary and poetry magazines that were otherwise difficult to place. While Borders was around, it completely distorted the market, which meant that smaller shops closed, caught between the big chains. Online buying was also a factor.

After Borders went belly-up, there was a black hole. People would come to us with new magazines, particularly literary and poetry titles, and we'd have to say 'We've got nowhere to put this.' The places we would have approached ten years ago didn't exist any more. The art magazines rode it all right: people bought them from the Tate, Institute of Contemporary Arts, Walther König. There were alternatives.

Since then there has been a partial recovery, in that some of the better outlets have seen it as an opportunity. The Fruitmarket Gallery in Edinburgh, which was located between a small Borders and the huge Glasgow Borders, trebled its magazine section. And new art bookshops popped up, like Artwords in Rivington Street, London.

In the UK, Foyles is an interesting success story. It has completely reinvented itself; it has taken on a nice, controlled selection of magazines; it has expanded. There are reasons to be cheerful – it's tough, it's tight, but it's not disastrous. We have a very good relationship with some key retailers in Europe: Athenaeum in Amsterdam, for example: a massive shop run by people who really love magazines and choose them very carefully. Also, Do You Read Me in Berlin is a lovely shop run by two people who take it very seriously and monitor their stock carefully. That is the key to success in shops: people who love what they do.

2. Checking off titles at Central Books, London

Getting it out there

06

A step-by-step guide
to distribution

What approach is
right for your title?

Logistics and
getting paid

DIY distribution
and direct sales

Alternative routes
to market

Subscription pros
and cons

How to get your magazine into readers' hands: from distribution and subscriptions to do-it-yourself and selling direct

You've planned it, written it, designed it and printed it, and issue one of your magazine is sitting in boxes – under your bed, stacked in your studio or on a palette at the printer. Where they need to be is in shops or, better still, in readers' hands. How do you get them there? Welcome to the dark art of distribution.

Distribution is the most commonly cited problem among independent magazine publishers, and the smaller you are, the harder it is. The financial return from sales is comparatively small with professional distribution, an industry that is generally still geared towards the traditional publishing model of larger commercial publishers – a high turn-over of cheaper products, with room for wastage.

The choice of whether to use a professional distribution company or to do it yourself hinges on your model and the size of your operation. Infrequent magazines with a small print run might be able to handle relationships with retailers themselves, but that level of micromanagement on your behalf means serious wo/man hours bashing the phone, negotiating deals, chasing invoices from each and every retailer and shipping or personally carrying magazines to shops. You might decide that your time is better spent creating content or wooing advertisers.

'Distribution needs to change in the coming years to respond to the growing number of independent magazines,' observes the publisher of *Disegno*, Johanna Agerman Ross. 'I admire the way some magazines are trying to do distribution differently, but, having looked at it carefully, I know how time-consuming it is and I prefer to stick with models that I know will get the magazine out there … I still think there's a large group of people who like to see it in a shop and flick through before they decide to make a purchase.'

Bigger print runs and/or a time-poor team will make a distributor essential. Bryony Lloyd of Antenne Books, a distribution company in London, reckons that the tipping point for a title needing a distributor is when it prints about 1,000 copies. 'A thousand copies is a lot to be sending out yourself,' she says. 'More than that and it will start taking up your whole life.'

Ultimately, opting to use a distributor is a faster way of increasing your circulation, and therefore your print run. It gets your magazine under more noses and multiplies your on-shelf presence, and although you make little money from sales, you are much more visible. Professional distribution is a promotional tool that will build your profile faster than DIY distribution, and bigger circulation gives you greater traction with advertisers.

Read on to discover the benefits and costs of using a distributor and how to incorporate it into your publishing model.

1.

1. A selection of magazines distributed by Antenne Books

Finding a professional distributor

It is your distributor's job to promote your title to the right retailers, monitor and adjust supply according to demand, and collect payment for you from retailers. You will get a percentage of the cover price for any copies sold in this way. Some distributors offer fixed percentages, others will negotiate. Depending on the deal, you can expect to earn about 30–50 per cent of the cover price after a cut has been taken by the retailer and the distributor. This varies from distributor to distributor, and your bargaining power depends on your size; the smaller your print run, the less earning power, and thus bargaining power, you have.

Keep talking to your distributor. A good, helpful one will tailor its service to your needs, but take it upon yourself to keep the channels of communication open, asking for feedback on sales figures and for advice on maximizing efficiency. As an independent title, one of your selling points is quality, which means high production values; unsold copies, therefore, are not only heartbreaking but also deeply inefficient. Copies of your magazine that are unsold by retailers will either be sent back to be pulped or have their covers ripped off (as proof of unsold numbers, on which the retailer will get a refund).

Don't forget to budget for the cost of sending your magazines to the distributor. You'll have to cover that yourself, or arrange it with your printer, who will charge a fee to deliver to specified addresses.

See page 142 about specifying print Once the distributor has your consignment of copies, it should take care of the cost of shipping to retailers.

In recent years, a handful of new-breed distributors have emerged, responding to the surge in small-scale indie publishing. Outfits like Antenne Books in London and Motto in Berlin are attuned to the needs of independent magazine-makers. They're small companies themselves, run by small teams, and you'll get a much more personal service than with bigger distributors. If your model is based on advertising and volume, however, a larger distribution company might offer greater coverage, but will probably be less attentive to the fine detail.

You might use several different distribution companies, each offering a different kind of service or geographical focus. For example, you might need one company to distribute magazines in Europe and another for the United States. One company might specialize in bookshops, and another in newsagents and news-stands.

"This is the non-sexy part."

Andrew Diprose, *The Ride Journal*

Size matters: intelligent formats

Noon

Date launched: Spring 2014
Location: United Kingdom
Print run: 4,000
Size: 240 x 340 mm (9½ x 12½ in)
Number of pages: 160
Weight per copy: 960 g (2 lb 2 oz)

Noon is a large, thick biannual magazine showcasing art and fashion photography. The production values are second to none, using high-quality, weighty paper stocks and expansive layouts to show off beautifully printed visuals. 'The format of *Noon* was chosen to adhere to the most common photographic image dimensions,' says its founder and editor-in-chief, Jasmine Raznahan, 'so as not to have to crop any full-bleed images unnecessarily. It felt practical and was ultimately informed by the content.' *Noon* is distributed to bookshops and art-gallery shops, and is designed to make a big statement on the shelf. It uses a distribution company to sell through retailers and news-stands.

Works That Work

Date launched: February 2013
Location: The Netherlands
Print run: 5,500
Size: 170 x 240 mm (6¾ x 9½ in)
Number of pages: 92
Weight per copy: 100 g (3.5 oz)

Also published twice a year, the format of the diminutively proportioned *Works That Work* is all about portability, to maximize the innovative system of 'social distribution' it has pioneered as part of its publishing model. 'It was designed so that a stack of ten weighs 1 kg,' says its founder, Peter Bil'ak. 'So to take ten copies with you in your luggage is really no effort. All these small things – making sure the weight of the magazine was right, that it is portable, the choice of stocks and papers – it's all part of the design.' Most copies are sold either directly through its website or via social distribution, where readers buy copies at a discount to sell to local retailers or friends.

Getting paid

It's important to remember that when using a distributor you have to wait for payment. Depending on the distributor and the frequency of your magazine, this could be anything from one to three months after one issue has come off sale and been replaced by the next. Plan your cash flow accordingly.

See Chapter 8, Money talks, about financial planning and cash flow

As the publisher, you're the last in the queue to get paid. The distributor requests sales reports from the retailer (generally quarterly); when it has established the number of copies sold, you will receive a report, after which you can issue an invoice to the distributor. Invoices generally have 30-day payment terms, so under such an arrangement you should receive payment of your percentage of the copies sold about four months after you supplied them.

If you produce a quarterly magazine, therefore, you cannot count on revenue from issue 1 before you have to pay for production of issue 2.

> **"Magazines in your garage are not great, magazines in the hands of readers – especially if they have paid some money for them – are fantastic."**
>
> **Simon Esterson, *Eye***

DIY distribution

+ **It's cheaper** because you cut out the distributor's percentage and the cover price is divided between you and the retailer

+ **You can build the business gradually** with a fairly clear idea of your revenue for each issue – which is great if you're starting small

+ **You usually get paid faster** than if you use a distributor (although this can vary)

– **It's a big investment** of time and effort to keep track of each individual retailer relationship

– **It might take longer** to build your profile and your readership

Professional distribution

+ **Free up your time to make the magazine** by handing the process over to someone else

+ **Get readers you might not otherwise reach,** build your profile and readership faster

+ **A fast route to bigger circulation,** which will help you to sell your title to advertisers

– **It's more expensive** and you'll have less of a profit margin than if you sell direct to readers

– **You're the last in the chain to be paid,** which affects cash flow

– **You will lose unsold copies**

A step-by-step guide to the distribution process

All distribution companies work slightly differently,
but this covers the standard elements of the process.

1 Approach distributors you'd like to work with, either with a copy of your magazine, if you have made it already, or with information and mock-ups (check individual distributors' specifications for how they like to receive pitches).

2 Strike a deal and exchange contracts with your distributor, including an agreement on what percentage of the cover price you'll get from each magazine sold, and payment terms.

3 Your distributor will promote your magazine to retailers and begin compiling a set of standing orders from a list of retailers that suit your title.

4 Send copies of your first issue to the distributor's warehouse.

5 The distributor will ship copies to the individual retailers and invoice them (the retailer usually pays the distributor within 30 days). Your magazine is on sale.

6 Three months after the magazine has gone on sale, the distributor prepares a quarterly report, based on feedback from the retailers about how many copies have sold.

7 You can then send your invoice to the distributor, with the standard 30 days' payment terms, for your share of the cover price on copies sold.

8 You get paid (three months + 30 days after your magazine went on sale).

Pet projects and day-job spin-offs

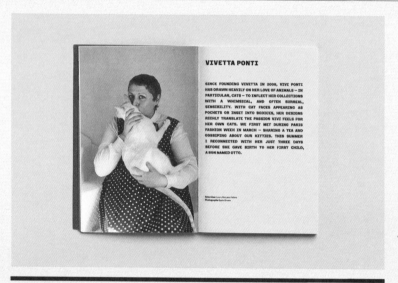

Cat People

Frequency: Annual
Date launched: September 2013
Location: Melbourne, Australia
Print run: 1,000
Cover price: AU$30

Cat People is a bilingual (English/Japanese) magazine featuring exclusive interviews and work by cat-obsessed artists, designers, photographers and writers. Using a mixture of avenues for sales, including its own website, direct relationships with retailers and distribution companies for both Australia and New Zealand (Perimeter) and the United Kingdom and Europe (Antenne Books), *Cat People* typifies the multichannel approach of small indie titles. 'The idea behind *Cat People* grew from our love of Japanese books and publishing, which inspired us with their delicate balance of niche subject matter and ambitious production,' say its makers, the designer Jessica Lowe and photographer Gavin Green.

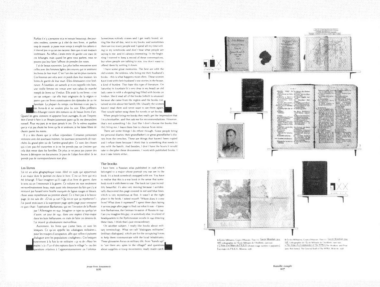

The Shelf Journal

Frequency: Biannual
Date launched: February 2012
Location: Paris
Print run: 1,500
Cover price: €20

The Shelf Journal is run by the French graphic designers Morgane Rébulard and Colin Caradec as a playground for their obsession with beautiful printed matter. Opting out of traditional distribution, they instead gradually built up a network of contacts in book and magazine shops to supply directly. They did this in their own way and on their own, searching out the right contacts and talking to them about the project. The magazine 'washes its face' financially, but does not earn its creators a living. 'The magazine has its own economic balance,' they say. 'Money from the previous issue allows us to print the next one … We run an art-direction studio, which is what we really do for a living.'

DIY distribution

If giving 40–60 per cent of your cover price to a professional distributor is something you just can't stomach, or if it simply doesn't make financial sense – often the case for new magazines starting small and looking to build slowly – there are other routes.

You might start out doing distribution yourself and then move on to a professional distribution company once you hit a level of sales that means you need help to maintain relationships with retailers. That is the approach taken by Polly Glass and Chris Harrison, makers of *Wrap* magazine, which was launched in 2010. '*Wrap*'s funded by our readers, with revenue coming purely from sales rather than from advertising or sponsored content,' says Glass. 'We've been able to take this approach by being careful to build demand steadily. To begin with, we did all the distribution in-house, only selling to stockists on a firm-sale basis to be sure we would receive payment for all the copies we sent out. It was only when we reached a certain level of sales that we were able to switch to a more traditional model and use specialist magazine distributors.'

Don't be shy about dealing with retailers in a way that makes financial sense for you. When Rosa Park and Rich Stapleton launched *Cereal* in 2012, they struck direct deals with shops they really wanted to be stocked in based on firm sales, rather than 'sale or return' or selling 'on consignment'. 'I think because magazines are low-risk products in terms of price,' says Park, 'a lot of stores were more than happy to give it a go as long as they liked the feel and look of the title. I would send them preview PDFs to check out. I rarely sent out sample copies, just because we didn't have the budget … but I did make exceptions for stores I truly, truly wanted to be in.'

Sale or return means that you send your magazines to the retailer and, after an agreed period, they will pay you for copies sold and return any unsold copies.

'On consignment' essentially means the same thing. You supply copies of your magazine to the retailer, which sells them on your behalf. You can then invoice, at a pre-agreed price, for copies sold.

Discounting, which is expected by retailers, means that you sell your copies to them at a discount. This is negotiable, but magazines are usually sold to retailers at a discount of 25–30 per cent (meaning a considerably better cut for you than you get using a distributor).

Don't forget, when costing your options, that you need to factor in the cost of shipping copies to retailers. This can get expensive when you're sending large packets overseas, so do your research.

2.

2. London-based distributor Antenne Books' pop-up store at Melk gallery in Oslo

3. Alternative magazine distribution company Stack holds regular events where readers can hear magazine experts speak and sample new titles

4. IndieCon 2015 in action, featuring displays and products from independent publishers around the world

3.

4.

DIY direct sales

Selling copies yourself, direct to readers, guarantees you the best margins. But you need to be proactive and drum up business by driving traffic to your online shopfront. Social media is a powerful tool here, as is an email database of people to whom you can send newsletters.

See page 145 for ideas about promotion and publicity

Some publishers create hype around the launch of a new issue by offering a pre-order service, which also brings in cash to make an issue before it goes to print. Readers get the chance to pay upfront to reserve their copy, perhaps in return for a reduced price or an added extra like an add-on product. This is especially effective if you have a healthy online readership and you bill your print title as a must-have, 'limited-edition' product.

When it comes to taking payment, there are a number of third-party selling tools you can use rather than forking out for a bespoke e-commerce system. Some, such as PayPal and Stripe, allow you to integrate payment buttons and features into your existing website. Others, such as Big Cartel, are external marketplaces that can host a page linked to your site.

Your website is also a place to promote subscriptions and back issues, to emphasize the collectibility of your title.

As well as selling copies online, consider getting out in the world to sell copies face-to-face with your readers at industry events.

"Sell as many copies as you can yourself, that way you get all the money!"

Luke Wood, *Head Full of Snakes*

Dedicated DIY-ers

Gym Class

Frequency: Ad hoc: 'I try to aim for two or three per year'
Date launched: November 2009
Print run: 250
Cover price: Variable; approximately £6
Magazine in three words: Magtastic, fanboy, aceness

A real labour of love, *Gym Class* is run as a personal project by the designer Steven Gregor. It's a magazine about magazines, and has something of a cult following in the mag world. Despite being small, *Gym Class* has included contributions from the leading lights of international publishing. Its format and design change from issue to issue, and every page oozes Gregor's personal enthusiasm for his subject. It is a true DIY project, and he does everything himself, including distributing the magazine. Asked what questions any aspiring magazine-maker should consider, Gregor says: 'How will I get my magazine in front of the right audience? Distribution is tricky, expensive and time-consuming.'

Head Full of Snakes

Frequency: Annual
Date launched: January 2012
Print run: 1,000
Cover price: AU$15–20
Magazine in three words:
Manual labour, obsessiveness

The project of designers Luke Wood and Stuart Geddes, based in New Zealand and Australia, the motorbike super-fanzine *Head Full of Snakes* began life as a project funded by Canterbury University, New Zealand, 'as a research outcome, and a publication that would investigate the politics of manual labour through the guise of a motorcycle magazine'. To the makers' surprise, it was very well received and won awards. 'Since the [beginning] we have produced each issue with money made from sales of the previous one,' say Wood and Geddes. It is distributed almost exclusively via the *Head Full of Snakes* website and 'the occasional bookstore also, if you're lucky!'

Subscriptions

Holy grail or poisoned chalice? Subscriptions are a commitment, both for you as publisher and for your customer. Offering subs means entering into an ongoing economic relationship with your readers: they pay you upfront for a year's worth (or two) of magazines and you, in turn, have to honour that commitment to supply the goods.

On the one hand, this is brilliant. You have the cash in your bank account to fund the making of future issues, you have committed buyers and you can flash those statistics to potential advertisers. You also pocket a much higher percentage of the cover price than you would on copies sold by retailers. But, as with any good relationship, you also have to put the effort in. The money might be in the bank, but there are extra bills to pay, and you need to be careful with cash flow, ensuring there are funds to make copies of your magazine for the duration of all your 'live' subscriptions.

Then there's the admin. If you're offering subscriptions, people can take them out at any point in your publishing cycle, and you need a way to keep track of every single subscriber, when their subscription starts and how many copies are left on each subscription. You've got to collect payments and stay in touch – let each person know how long their subscription has to run, remind them when it's coming to an end and deal with feedback ('Where's my latest issue?!'). You might have 1,000 individual subscribers, each with a different start and end point to their subscription. This is, of course, much easier to manage if you are a biannual magazine than if you are a monthly.

Don't forget to factor in the cost of postage. Using a fulfilment service can be cheaper than posting individual copies yourself, but beware the cost of sending subscriptions overseas. These can be off-puttingly expensive for customers, and can take a big chunk out of your margin if you intend to subsidize postage costs yourself. You might be better off considering a distribution service for overseas locations.

5. Subscribers to *Delayed Gratification* find that each issue arrives in a special slip case; they can also get priority tickets for the magazine's Slow Journalism events

Subscription services

There are a number of ways you can run your subscriptions. The one you choose depends on the volume of subscriptions you have to manage and how much time you have on your hands.

▶ **Do it yourself** Start small and be super-organized – you'll need systems for handling customers' information, processing payments and sending out copies.

▶ **Fulfilment** The next step up is to farm out aspects of the process to an order fulfilment company. You can choose various levels of service, from a simple store-and-send service, where you supply magazines and a list of subscribers; or you can pay them to handle everything from taking payments and updating your subscriber database, to delivery and customer returns.

▶ **Subscriptions companies** are specialists in complete fulfilment (see above) and will handle the whole process. They can also provide digital order systems linked to your own website to process orders and automatically update your database. Costly, but if you are publishing more than a couple of times per year and have several thousand subscribers, it's probably essential.

▶ **Subscriptions consultants** can be hired freelance to manage the relationship with your fulfilment or subscriptions supplier, monitor the day-to-day process, increase efficiency and devise and implement promotional campaigns.

5.

Design and incentives

Subscriptions are all about loyalty, and it's important to reward your readers for choosing to pay upfront. Every subscriber copy is a little ambassador for your magazine and what it stands for. The way you package those copies should convey the level of quality and attention to detail that you put into every other aspect of making your magazine: each copy should elicit a flutter of excitement and anticipation as it is unwrapped.

You can do this very simply with well-designed carrier sheets (the sheet of paper printed with the address that is inserted by your subscription handler or fulfilment house) or go to town with bespoke wrapping and boxes. Speak to your fulfilment or subscriptions company about your options – it's worth being persistent if you want something out of the ordinary.

Subscriptions give you the best profit margins on copy sales so it's worth promoting them as much as possible. Try running targeted discount offers, for example at events or with partners. As well as promoting them online look at options such as placing promotional cards in other publications with a target audience you want to reach.

> "My top advice to anyone selling subscriptions is to use the GoCardless service for taking direct debits. It's cheap, easy and will bring your churn rate right down. I wish it had existed when we first launched!"
>
> **Rob Orchard,** *Delayed Gratification*

Subscriptions

+ **Money in the bank upfront** to fund future issues

+ **Loyal readers** and guaranteed print run are appealing to advertisers

− **Time, effort and/or cost** of managing subscriptions

− **Financial liability and responsibility** to deliver the magazines that have been paid for

Join the club: hooking subscribers

Monocle

Frequency: 10 per year
Print run: 80,000
Cover price: £7
Annual subscription price:
From £100
Copy sales: 80 per cent
news-stand/shop; 20 per cent
subscription

Monocle, 'a briefing on global affairs, business, culture and design' founded by the much-admired publishing guru Tyler Brûlé, operates with a large editorial staff at its headquarters, Midori House in Marylebone, London. It also has bureaux in seven other cities around the world, and hundreds of contributing writers, researchers, photographers and illustrators. But *Monocle*'s brand can in essence be traced back to the clear and uncompromising vision of its publisher: it is an extension of Brûlé himself, from the magazine's scope and tone of voice to the smallest button on the soft furnishings at Midori House. Subscriptions are not discounted, but exclusive 'extras' are offered with each copy.

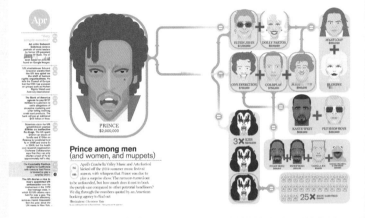

Prince among men
(and women, and muppets)

Delayed Gratification

Frequency: Quarterly
Print run: 6,000–7,000
Cover price: £10
Annual subscription price:
From £36
Copy sales: 40 per cent
news-stand/shop; 60 per cent
subscription

Subscribers to *Delayed Gratification* are treated to a tangible process of discovery every time an issue arrives, housed in its printed box and special slip case. The process of receiving and unwrapping the object underlines the values of quality and careful attention to detail that are applied to every element of the title's design and editorial. 'The key [has always been] selling subscriptions rather than single issues,' says its co-founder, Rob Orchard. 'Since the idea [of slow journalism, pioneered by the title] resonated with so many people, we were able to sell year-long subscriptions, which gave us the working capital we needed to get the ball rolling.'

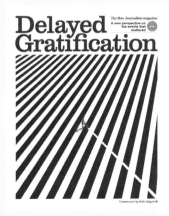

Alternative routes

Online magazine kiosks and selling tools are worth considering as distribution methods with a better margin for you than traditional distributors. A service like newsstand.co.uk will take a consignment of your magazines, promote it through its online shop and simply charge you a set fee for each copy sold. The fee is based on the weight of your magazine.

With magpile.com, you can create an online shopfront that you can link to from your website or use to embed 'buy' buttons that lead to your website. It is also an online shop where customers can browse magazines and buy single issues or subscriptions. It's a bit different from other distributors in that you have to fulfil (package and post) orders yourself, but the fees and discounts are much smaller (a monthly fee of about £6 and a charge for each copy sold of 8 per cent of the cover price at the time of writing). You can fix your own postage charges and they will be paid to you in full along with the remainder of the cover price.

The subscription service Stack, run by magazine expert Steven Watson, has helped to boost the fortunes of many independent magazines. Each month subscribers receive a different indie title from an ever-growing selection curated by Watson, helping magazines to reach a new audience that might not otherwise be accessible.

Watson invites magazines to participate, and the publisher plans ahead to print about 3,000 extra copies, which Watson buys for about £1.60 per copy and sends to Stack subscribers. 'The publisher prints the extra copies, and treats them as a "run-on" to what they'd normally be printing,' Watson explains. 'That brings the unit cost down (to a matter of pence in a lot of cases) and means they make a profit even though they're giving Stack an unprecedented discount ... I pay as soon as the magazines hit my warehouse, so there's no waiting around for the money to come in from news-stands, and of course there's no sale or return, so there's really no risk at all to the publisher.'

> **"Online sales are far more profitable than news-stand, but the latter act as a source of new readers that feeds into the former."**
>
> **Liz Ann Bennett,** *Oh Comely*

Read about the ingenious invention of social distribution pioneered by *Works That Work* magazine on pages 91 and 146–51

6.

6. Stack's magazine subscription service rewards indie publishers by introducing them to new readers

Routes to readers

Oh Comely

Frequency: Bi-monthly
Print run: 15,000
Number of in-house staff: Three full-time; three part-time
Number of pages: 132

When *Oh Comely* was launched in 2010, it redrew the perimeters of women's lifestyle magazines, taking an honest, funny and thoughtful approach and eschewing the conventions of magazines aimed at young women. Its revenue streams are magazine sales – both direct sales online and shop/news-stand sales through a number of distribution partners; advertising; and creative agency services. Visibility and a wide reach are important for the title: as well as distributors to supply magazine shops and news-stands, including the high-street giant WHSmith, *Oh Comely* sells outside standard retail environments: in branches of Whole Foods and Anthropologie, airport lounges, Eurostar trains and educational institutions.

Offscreen

Frequency: 3 or 4 issues per year
Print run: 4,500
Number of in-house staff: One full-time
Distribution: 25 per cent international shops; 75 per cent direct online
Number of pages: 154

The mercurial editor, art director and publisher of *Offscreen* magazine, Kai Brach, is the quintessential one-man-band magazine-maker, and uses his own bespoke systems to organize distribution. He set up his title after years working in the digital world, to tell the stories and share the experiences of 'the people behind the bits and pixels'. Brach uses a custom-built order-management system that he developed with a friend to process orders from his website, shipping information for his fulfilment company, payments and subscriptions. He is candid about the process of publishing his magazine, and writes a regular blog about his methods, experiments and finances.

Hand-in-hand with the boom in independent magazines has been the rise of the independent magazine shop. As well as being places where the growing audience of magazine buyers go for their fix, they have also become hubs where publishers meet the readership through events. Meet Marc Robbemond, the buyer responsible for deciding what goes on the shelves at legendary magazine store Athanaeum Nieuwscentrum in Amsterdam.

1.

What are the ingredients you look for in a new title that might do well in your shop?
We have 2,000 titles in the shop. A strong identity is very important. I really appreciate it if a magazine picks up a topic that [its creators] are really interested in themselves, instead of just wanting to make a magazine because it's hip or cool at the moment. That's the foremost thing – the topic and the relationship of the makers to the topic. You can easily see that by reading a few articles.

In the shop, we have specialist sections: design, food, interior design, urbanism and architecture, literature, fashion, art, photography, biking, film and current affairs. So a new magazine also has to fit in to one of those areas.

What proportion of magazines in the shop are independently published?
At the moment the collection is 40 per cent independent, which is big. Although the general magazine landscape is mostly commercial – large publishers who work with a lot of advertising – there has been a big shift over the last six years. The number of indie titles is really going up. In terms of sales, the independent magazines are doing very well.

Interview
The Retailer

Marc Robbemond
Retailer, Athenaeum
Nieuwscentrum, Amsterdam

2.

What is encouraging that independent scene?

I think now people are more interested in the analogue thing, in collecting magazines. I recently read somewhere that it's the same fascination you get with the magazine scene that people had with the indie music scene: you can collect and cherish and discover something that has a lot more relevance to you than a magazine that just wants to sell you something. The more commercial ones are just that – it's all based on advertising. The new magazines that go deeply into their subject are super-fascinating. It's almost as though you buy a book on one topic, but every three months there is a new chapter of the book coming out. Also, it's just super-hip. You can see that with the hipster scene and magazines like *Kinfolk* and *Cereal*.

That has been a big trend, the new breed of lifestyle mag. But what are the new emerging trends?

The last couple of months [October 2014] we've seen a lot of new erotic magazines that are very arty. They are not so far away from the *Kinfolk* trend because the aesthetic is very calm, not so raw. But at the moment, design-wise, some more raw publications are coming out, a reaction to the white spaces of the last couple of years. Maybe now people want something that fills the pages and is not so calm all the time.

There have been a lot of followers of that considered, very tasteful style, but do you think people now want more of a punk feeling, a more 'zine-like aesthetic?

Yes, something that is not so perfect and idealistic. I think a title like *Another Escape* is just outside that scene, a little more raw. Also *Oak: The Nordic Journal*, for example, a Norwegian/Swedish magazine. It's not so much that these are imitations, but rather people who are inspired by that scene. Sometimes we think we could stock them all, but then you have a magazine shop with only these calm magazines. It's nice to see something different.

What does it take to get a magazine stocked in Athenaeum Nieuwscentrum? Do you have to turn many publishers away?

The biggest part of rejection or refusal of a title is because the distribution is not profitable. It's very difficult for us to import titles from the US [since] it's very expensive to send it and then we have to add shipping costs to the cover price. Sometimes people are willing to pay quite a high price for a specialist magazine; €25 is common at the moment, but some go up to €30 or €35 and then it's too risky. You don't want to have this pile of overly expensive magazines in the store that no one buys. When that's the case, I try to connect the publishers with European distributors like Antenne Books in London or Motto in Berlin.

On the whole, we like to give magazine-makers a chance. Sometimes you don't know if a title will work, or it might not suit your personal tastes, but then we sell a big pile and have to order more. There's no magic formula.

1. Marc Robbemond, photograph by Ivan Jones

2. The Athenaeum Nieuwscentrum shopfront

Do you deal only with magazines who use a distributor?
No, we work directly with many small publishers. With independent magazines it's about 40 per cent distributors and 60 per cent direct, so there is a lot of work for me to deal with all the invoices and sending copies back and so on. At the same time it's nice to be in contact with the editors and publishers.

Distribution seems to be the biggest headache for indie publishers. Is there a tipping point when it becomes necessary for a small publisher to have a distributor?
I'm always happy when a magazine moves to a distributor because for me, as a retailer, it's so much easier: I can order bigger quantities and I can send back unsold copies much more easily. But I'm very well aware that, with payment structures and the percentage they get, it's not really profitable for the magazine-makers.

We still do direct deals with some makers who have a distributor, and I don't really mind that because, although it's a bit more work for us, I understand that they really need the percentage and the money for the next issue. The money is important for the magazine to go on existing, and it must be paid before the next issue goes to print. That's what you don't get with distributors; they pay later, when they have a clear view of what has sold and what has not sold.

A couple of times a year I collect all unsold copies from one distributor and send them back, and then we get a credit invoice. When we're ordering directly from an individual magazine, it works the same way, but I have to communicate everything to the makers myself. We take magazines on consignment ['sale or return'].

3.

What factors affect a magazine's sales performance?
It's something I'm always thinking about when I'm in the shop. An issue doesn't seem to be going well, but then it gets some publicity and we don't have enough copies and I have to order more. Sometimes a magazine that is always popular will have a new issue that isn't popular at all. It could even just be because of the cover, which seems a small thing but has a big influence on sales. Or sales might be affected because there's an issue of another magazine in the same field that is more exciting.

With independent magazines, I check stock levels frequently to make sure that we have enough in store. If we have just a few copies, I order more, because if there's a pile it attracts more attention. That process is going on all the time.

How do people make a magazine that will succeed in the mid- to long term?
By being super-distinctive and choosing a topic that you know you will find interesting over a long period. Those are the magazines that are succeeding. For example, *The Outpost*, which just published issue 5, has a strong concept: there will be a lot to write about the Middle East and the possibilities for the Middle East in the coming years. The makers don't have to worry about their concept; it will be interesting for a long time. *Flaneur* picks one street in one city and makes an

issue about the stories they find there. Also *Delayed Gratification* has a very strong concept, in which they can really frame their work with every issue.

I think working with a distributor as a small magazine will not give you much money, but it will get you attention. Stores don't have to discover you; your magazine will be presented to them. That is something to consider: OK, you don't make money, but if you get represented well at book fairs and in small shops then you get more spread, and that's something you want to do, to build up an audience. That is very important.

Is it a good idea for makers to consult retailers in that development stage? What can you advise on?

I can give a clue as to how many I would like to order. I can say that I would order ten copies on consignment, and if it goes well I will order more according to the speed of the sales. Also, I can say whether I like the concept and find it interesting as an addition to the store.

What about magazine frequency? Is there a trend towards magazines that are on sale for longer?

Yes, there are more biannuals. Also, more and more titles are changing from quarterly to biannual, which has to do with money and time. People often have jobs next to their magazine to support. As well as that, if you have a small team, the most important thing is to have consistent quality and new ideas. You don't want people to [pick up] a new issue and think: 'I've seen it before, and don't want to buy it again.' It has to be really good each time, so if you have half a year to prepare an issue you can go into a subject more deeply without the stress of adding articles that, afterwards, you realize didn't really make the issue stronger.

You hold regular magazine events at Athenaeum Nieuwscentrum. Is that a growing part of independent magazine culture?

We present new issues of magazines in the store. We love to do it with the makers and editors, whom we interview live. People are super-interested in hearing what they have to say. It's part of this new scene. We presented the art issue of *Colors* in the store, and the audience was very broad – people who were into art but also a lot of journalists. People are really interested in hearing how the editors and publishers make a magazine, in asking them questions and having a discussion about what is going on with magazines and how they see the future of print.

That's a topic that keeps on running …

People say print is not dead, obviously, but then we have to ask, what is its future? We don't know yet, but I think it will go on for a long time because so many print magazines are coming up and so many are also well established. There are magazines that come up and disappear, but in the meantime there are many titles that are really the heart of the shop. Plus there is a sense of community in the independent magazine world, and we're happy to be a part of that.

3. Magazine display at Athenaeum Nieuwscentrum

Advertising

07

A companion through the tricky terrain of advertising

The subject of advertising elicits mixed feelings from those in the independent publishing world. This is partly because indie publishers set themselves apart in many ways from the traditional publishing model, and some see advertising as a hangover from that mode of financing a magazine. In large-scale corporate publishing, magazines are set up entirely as a vehicle for advertising, and money from advertising sales is by far the biggest revenue stream.

In the independent world, magazine publishers value editorial pages in a different way, often because the publishers are also the editors and designers, whose priority is the reader, not the advertiser. Some independent magazines opt to eschew advertising revenue altogether, relying solely on the income from copy sales. If they do carry advertising, it might be somewhat of a 'necessary evil', or tightly controlled by being framed in a particular visual context. Other independent publishers, however, regard relationships with advertisers as something extremely positive. They recognize that selling just one page of advertising can bring in the same amount of cash as selling thousands of individual copies, and that, in some cases, advertising artwork can be as beautiful as a page of editorial, adding to the reader's experience.

Ultimately, your choice will depend on your publishing model and the scale of your ambitions. This chapter will help you to decide if advertising is right for you, give some examples of existing magazines' approaches, and offer practical tips for getting – and keeping – advertisers.

"If you're fierce, it's easy."

Dan Crowe, *Port*

Advertising checklist

For a publishing model that depends on advertising revenue, you need:

✔ A high-quality product

✔ A clear and unique editorial vision

✔ A well-defined readership

✔ A subject area with links to an advertising market

✔ A circulation of 10,000+

✔ Persistence and a great media pack (see pages 117–20)

Is advertising right for you?

When Johanna Agerman Ross set up the design magazine *Disegno* in 2011, it was planned carefully on a business model that included advertising. This was an ideological decision, as well as a business decision. 'I always wanted to see advertising as an integral part of the magazine,' she says. 'That's why it's more interesting to work with high-end brands who have a budget to produce beautiful campaigns – as a reader you get more out of that. I've never had anything against [advertising]; I've never wanted to create a magazine without it. I've always seen it as something that goes together with editorial. You just have to curate it carefully in order for it to sit well.'

Read a full interview with Johanna Agerman Ross on pages 32–37

Read the full interview with Peter Bil'ak on pages 146–51

For Peter Bil'ak, founder of *Works That Work*, however, advertising is at odds with his motivations for publishing and his aims for the magazine. Now, he insists, is a good time to look at alternatives, but it means redesigning the entire publishing model, from production to distribution.

The beauty of independence is that you can choose the road you're most comfortable with, so the route you choose for your own magazine might come down to principle, or to hard financial choices. If you make money by partnering with brands, how will that sit with your readership? Can you run ads that will be of genuine interest to your readers? Or is advertising completely discordant with your editorial aims? Does your subject area have a clear advertising market to partner with?

If you want to carry advertising, it could come through your close ties to an advertising market. A small title like *The Ride Journal*, for example, can sell enough advertising pages to pay for its print and paper bill every issue because there are plenty of brands in its field – cycling – that are ready to buy pages that appeal to a small but very engaged audience.

Alternatively, you might have a unique editorial offering that appeals to brands in a sector like fashion. Despite their size, enlightened global brands might recognize the power of partnering with a very focused, high-quality title.

"Advertisers just want to be associated with something that makes sense."

Matt Willey, *Port*

Advertising

+ **High yield revenue** compared to revenue from copy sales

+ **Fast, firm cash** to spend on production or other costs

+ **Good brand associations** can be an asset to your offering to readers

— **Brands must be palatable** to and appreciated by your audience

— **Advertisers may expect editorial presence** that compromises you

— **Pressure to find and broker advertiser relationships** for every issue, when you're commited to an advertising-funded model

Or, of course, you will need the power of numbers on your side. *The Gentlewoman* prints more than 90,000 copies, and has a very clearly defined editorial stance, putting it in a serious league that attracts advertising from global brands like Ralph Lauren, Dior and Prada. Not many indie titles enjoy such healthy circulation figures, but, realistically, you need a circulation of at least 10,000–15,000 copies to enter into serious conversations with major brands.

Quality versus quantity

No matter the print run or subject of your magazine, quality is an essential factor if you're looking for advertisers, since brands want to be associated with a thing of value. Likewise, your readers don't want to be bombarded with pages of advertising that jar with your editorial. It is in the interests of you, your readers and your advertisers to choose partnerships carefully; that way, ads feel 'right' and everyone wins.

If you can't compete on sheer volume of readership, you can on the quality of your product and that of the people you reach. *Disegno* prints 20,000–30,000 copies per issue – an admirable circulation in the indie world, but nowhere near the volume associated with the traditional fashion press – and yet Saint Laurent pays for an advertisement on its outside back cover. Another design title, *Printed Pages*, runs to 5,000–6,000 copies per issue, but maintains an ongoing advertising relationship with clients like Comme des Garçons and Paul Smith.

Rosa Park and Rich Stapleton launched the travel and lifestyle title *Cereal* in 2012 and ran no advertising for the first year. Once their print run hit 15,000 copies, however, they realized that advertising was a viable way of funding the magazine. 'If you do your advertising right it can legitimize and enhance your content,' Park says. 'If these brands believe in what you're doing, especially if it's a very new title, [that's] something very reassuring.'

In his shared resource The Publishing Playbook, the independent publisher Danny Miller includes some excellent advice from YCN's Head of Partnerships, Dean Faulkner, on the subject of advertising. Both Miller and Faulkner have a wealth of experience through instrumental roles at creative agencies including Church of London, Human After All and YCN. On the right is Faulkner's take on working with media agencies to secure advertising.

In many cases, advertising is handled by a media agency (such as Carat, Mediacom, Vizeum or Mindshare), so it's not just a case of finding a relevant contact at the brand, but also knowing which agency books their ads.

If you can, invest in an agency directory like ALF. ALF lists which agencies represent which brand and which person handles which account. It also lists marketing contacts at brands directly, so it's a worthwhile investment (the most basic package is around £2,500).

Media agencies are roughly split into two categories – media planning and media buying. Planners form the overall campaign. Once the plan is in place, it's down to the buyers to secure the media space from media owners (magazines, online, TV, etc.). It's important to get on to the radar of the buyers handling the accounts of brands you're targeting. You'll be speaking to print buyers, and if you also sell ad space on an accompanying website, you'll want to speak to the digital buying team.

Because media agencies represent multiple brands, it's worth trying to network between contacts. When speaking to a media buyer, ask them if they think the magazine might be of interest to their colleagues representing any other brands and if they could potentially introduce you.

You should build a mailing list for all the contacts, at brands and at media agencies, who should regularly receive copies of the magazine.

– Dean Faulkner, YCN Head of Partnerships

Riposte

Frequency: Biannual
Date launched: 2013
Location: London
Print run: 7,000
Language: English

Another title that redefines gender-based publishing, *Riposte*'s strapline is 'a smart magazine for women'. Its founder, Danielle Pender, says: 'Our aim is to inspire through doing. We don't talk from a traditional women's perspective; rather, the achievements of the women we feature speak for themselves.' Pender realized that there was a gap in the market when she discovered she was reading magazines aimed at men, unable find a high-quality, interesting title for women that was not steeped in fashion and gossip. Her gradual and considered approach to advertising, partnering with a few carefully picked brands, reflects her respect for her readers.

Port

Frequency: Biannual (formerly quarterly)
Date launched: Spring 2011
Location: London
Print run: 73,000
Language: English, with syndicated Russian and Middle Eastern editions

With layouts to die for and top-quality writing, *Port* has raised the bar in the world of men's magazines. Conveying the team's considerable publishing experience, it serves up sophisticated editorial and refuses to conform to the commercialized conventions of the genre. Nonetheless, its business model depends on advertising. 'Magazines have become so dependent on advertising that the fun in editorial gets diminished,' says *Port*'s editor-in-chief, Dan Crowe. 'Thumb through *GQ* and you cannot find a single piece of editorial that has any integrity, that is disconnected from a financial relationship. What we do in Port is to mix that kind of behaviour – handsome men wearing clothes and advertisers supporting that – with features that are uncommercial and sometimes difficult to read. That's called content …'

Getting (and keeping) advertisers

If you've decided that advertising will be part of your publishing model, where do you start? The decision to include ads means that you create the pressure to keep the advertising cash rolling in from issue to issue. You will need to create, nurture and maintain relationships with brands, balancing their needs with yours. Be realistic about the time and effort it will take to secure advertisers. Are you strong within your niche? Will you be competing against other, more established indie magazines for the same advertisers? What is unique about your offering, and how will you sell your magazine's opportunity to brands?

Once you have your advertisers, you must nurture the relationship. 'It's [a case of] consistently working to give them the confidence that we are very serious and [reassuring them of] the quality of the readership they're reaching by working with us,' says Park. 'It's being very clear and honest in that. Understanding how to use your strengths – that's what helps us in advertising.'

1. *Works That Work* media kit

2. *Riposte* media kit

3. *Perdiz* media kit

How to approach advertisers

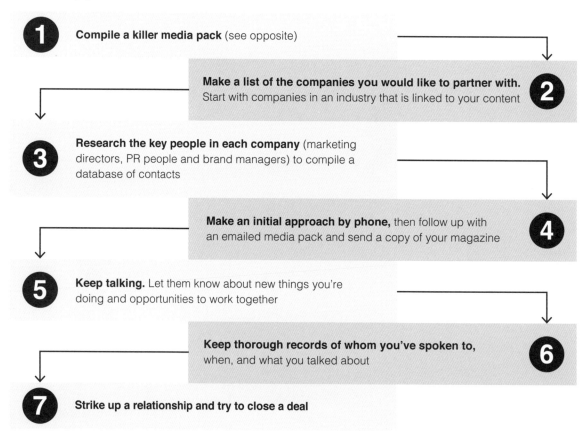

1 **Compile a killer media pack** (see opposite)

2 **Make a list of the companies you would like to partner with.** Start with companies in an industry that is linked to your content

3 **Research the key people in each company** (marketing directors, PR people and brand managers) to compile a database of contacts

4 **Make an initial approach by phone,** then follow up with an emailed media pack and send a copy of your magazine

5 **Keep talking.** Let them know about new things you're doing and opportunities to work together

6 **Keep thorough records of whom you've spoken to,** when, and what you talked about

7 **Strike up a relationship and try to close a deal**

Making a media pack

Whether you are selling direct to small businesses or approaching global brands through media agencies, you'll need a great media pack. This, your prime sales tool, will present all the information an advertiser will need to know in one handy place. It should be an ambassador for your title in every sense, channelling the look and feel of your magazine and accentuating your strengths and unique features. It could take the form of a printed document, a page on your website or a digital format such as PDF.

Media Kit

Works That Work is an international magazine for the curious mind, endeavouring to surprise its readers with a rich mix of diverse subjects connected by the theme of unexpected creativity that improves our lives. We publish original, in-depth essays and stories on subjects connected with design, presenting projects that challenge and change the way you perceive them. Perhaps most importantly, we hope to publish articles that make great dinner stories to tell your friends.

Introduction video
https://vimeo.com/84298331

Works That Work was awarded The Best New Magazine of 2013.
More information: Wtapple.com/awards

1.

Introduce the magazine

Sum up your editorial stance, what you stand for as a magazine and why you are unique in a simple paragraph. This is much easier said than done, but it's worth investing time in. Be pithy: *Works That Work* does it well with the line 'We hope to publish articles that make great dinner stories to tell your friends.'

Give some detail

What subjects do you explore and how do you approach them? Who are your contributors? What is special about the way your magazine is produced? What is your digital or online offering?

Visuals

Include your most striking and representative recent covers and spreads. Execute the design of your media pack with the level of quality, care and attention you apply to the magazine itself.

2.

3.

The opportunity

Explain to potential advertisers what they get out of having a presence in your title. This might be the key paragraph that unlocks your title for an advertiser. They will want to know what your readers respond to and how your magazine chimes with their brand. How do you offer one-of-a-kind access to the people the brand wants to reach?

Show off your accolades

If you've won recognition and awards in your industry, or received positive media coverage, include brief details or quotations.

4.

5.

Readership

What type of people read your magazine, and why? Outline the demographic, their interests and buying habits. Once you're up and running, a readership survey is a great way to get some hard facts into this section of the media pack.

Rate card

This is ostensibly your price list, but it is really a jumping-off point for negotiations. Most magazines offer discounts on the rate card to help close a sale or encourage multiple bookings. List the positions for sale (such as inside front cover, inside back cover, outside back cover, single pages, double-page spread). You might be able to offer deals on packages that include a combination of print and digital advertising. When you're researching how much to charge for advertising pages, it's worth looking at what other magazines charge. The range across the independent sector is vast. It's easy enough to find media kits and rate cards online for the magazines at the top end of the sector (*Monocle* and *The Gentlewoman*, for example), and at the smaller end, friendly fellow publishers might be willing to share their information with you if you ask nicely.

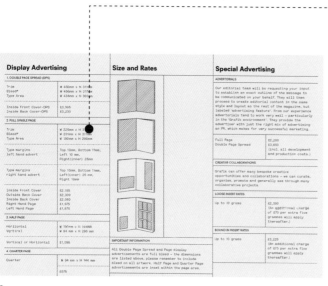

6.

7.

Collaborations, advertorials

Pitch the opportunities you offer outside on-page advertisements, such as sponsored sections, events and bespoke projects.

Publishing schedule

Media buyers often plan a year or more in advance, and have specific times of year when they allocate budgets for campaigns. Give them information about the dates of your future issues and what topics they will cover.

Contact details

Make it very easy for potential advertisers to talk to you about working together.

Vital statistics

Give bullet-point information about your magazine's print circulation, social media numbers, frequency, cover price, dimensions, page count and language.

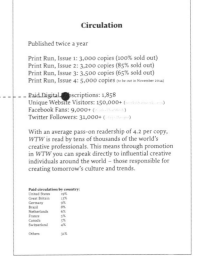

8.

Circulation

Published twice a year

Print Run, Issue 1: 3,000 copies (100% sold out)
Print Run, Issue 2: 3,200 copies (85% sold out)
Print Run, Issue 3: 3,500 copies (65% sold out)
Print Run, Issue 4: 5,000 copies (to be out in November 2014)

Paid Digital Subscriptions: 1,858
Unique Website Visitors: 150,000+ (worldthatwork.com)
Facebook Fans: 9,000+ (WorksThatWork)
Twitter Followers: 31,000+ (@typotheque)

With an average pass-on readership of 4.2 per copy, *WTW* is read by tens of thousands of the world's creative professionals. This means through promotion in *WTW* you can speak directly to influential creative individuals around the world – those responsible for creating tomorrow's culture and trends.

Paid circulation by country:

United States	19%
Great Britain	13%
Germany	9%
Brazil	8%
Netherlands	6%
France	5%
Canada	5%
Switzerland	4%
Others	31%

Distribution

You might want to summarize your distribution channels and what parts of the world you reach, or even include a full list of stockists.

9.

Formats, specifications

This is where you tell your advertisers about the positions and sizes you offer and explain any technical requirements for delivering their artwork to you. You might also want to include payment terms and your cancellation policy.

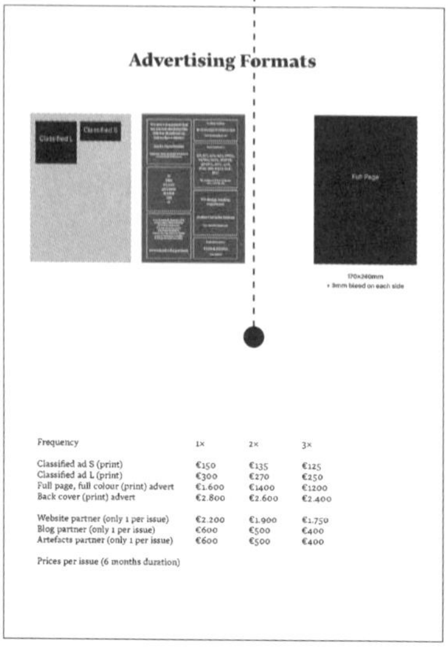

Advertising Formats

Frequency	1×	2×	3×
Classified ad S (print)	€150	€135	€125
Classified ad L (print)	€300	€270	€250
Full page, full colour (print) advert	€1.600	€1400	€1200
Back cover (print) advert	€2.800	€2.600	€2.400
Website partner (only 1 per issue)	€2.200	€1.900	€1.750
Blog partner (only 1 per issue)	€600	€500	€400
Artefacts partner (only 1 per issue)	€600	€500	€400

Prices per issue (6 months duration)

10.

Positioning advertisments

Most magazines avoid placing advertising pages in the middle of the publication, where it's all about engaging the reader in an uninterrupted reading and looking experience. Instead, ads are confined to the front and back sections, where articles are shorter, which means more opportunities to break up editorial with single pages of ads. The front and back are also where readers begin to flick from, so it's appealing to advertisers to stand out there.

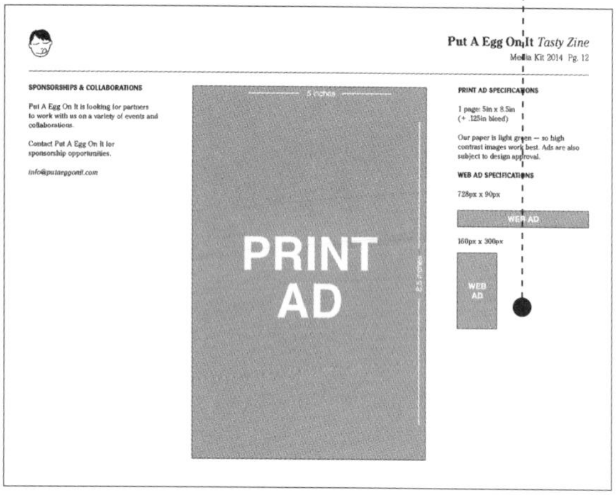

Put A Egg On It *Tasty Zine*
Media Kit 2014 Pg. 12

SPONSORSHIPS & COLLABORATIONS

Put A Egg On It is looking for partners to work with us on a variety of events and collaborations.

Contact Put A Egg On It for sponsorship opportunities.

info@putaeggonit.com

PRINT AD SPECIFICATIONS

1 page: 5in x 8.5in
(+ .125in bleed)

Our paper is light green — so high contrast images work best. Ads are also subject to design approval.

WEB AD SPECIFICATIONS

728px x 90px

160px x 300px

11.

Positions

Here is a guide to the common terms and abbreviations relating to standard advertising positions. These are for full-page ads, which are more common to indie magazines than 'classifieds'.

- **IFC** Inside front cover
- **Facing IFC**
- **Facing masthead**
- **Single page**
- **Page run of magazine** A page in an unspecified position
- **DPS** Double-page spread
- **IBC** Inside back cover
- **OBC** Outside back cover

Inventiveness and integrity

There are alternative ways of generating revenue from your relationships with brands than by simply selling pages in your publication. By being creative you can offer inventive routes for brands to reach your readers. Bespoke sponsored events can allow you to explore ideas that interest you editorially, appeal to your readers, and buy credibility and access to difficult-to-reach audiences for a brand.

The Gentlewoman collaborates with brands to lay on events for members of its readers' club, such as ghost walks and running groups. *Disegno* holds regular salons in partnership with brands, as well as generating ideas for bespoke events. 'For us, it's very important to have the independence to put our own stamp on [an event],' says its editor, Johanna Agerman Ross, 'or it's not worth putting our name to it. In those cases, working with brands, we can make what we already do … also beneficial for the business.'

You can even approach traditional on-page adverts in a fresh way to make them more compliant with your editorial vision, as Kai Brach has done in his magazine *Offscreen*. Advertisers pay for a 'sponsor's' page with a logo, link and paragraph of text treated in the standardized visual format of white logo and text out of a black page. Brach funds the production costs of each issue from these ad sales, along with 'patron' slots, for which he charges $100. He explains this approach on his blog:

12.

"Don't start with the Google of your industry, start with a company you already have close contacts with, maybe even a local one. Set your initial fee very low. Sponsoring the first issue of *Offscreen* cost $400 and barely made a dent in the cost of everything, but it helped establish a relationship with those companies. I got a chance to prove that *Offscreen* is a product worth investing in, and as a result many of those companies are still sponsoring the magazine today."

13.

As a publisher, you can also sell your creative resources to a brand, using your team and access to great contributors to make content for brands. This is something a lot of independent magazines do, and count as an essential part of their revenue. The team at *The Gentlewoman* designs and art-directs a magazine for the fashion retailer Cos; Human After All, the creative agency that publishes *Weapons of Reason*, has made publications for Google, Facebook and the World Economic Forum; and the makers of *Boat* magazine made a site-specific publication for the performing-arts organization LIFT's festival in Derry-Londonderry in 2014.

From his office at the top of Midori House in Marylebone, London, Tyler Brûlé presides over three floors packed with industrious, talented people: on the ground floor is Monocle 24, the magazine's in-house radio station; on the first floor is *Monocle* magazine itself; and on the second floor is Winkreative, the branding and contract publishing agency Brûlé opened between leaving *Wallpaper** in 2002 and launching *Monocle* in 2007. Here, he shares a wealth of wisdom from his unique vantage point within independent publishing.

1.

How did you construct the publishing model for *Monocle*?
We had the luxury of having done it once. If I think back to *Wallpaper**, it was a case of having absolutely no clue how to do it; having a passion to bring out a magazine, having this burning idea to bring this title to market, but really having no idea about the mechanics other than knowing that we had to sell advertising and knowing that it was going to be for an international audience. But [we had] no concept of how it should be financed, how the trajectory would look or how one builds a P&L [profit and loss statement].

It was a luxury to be able to make a series of mistakes and also then have the good fortune to sell the magazine after a year or two to Time Warner, and then still run it for five years within the corporate environment. I look back on *Wallpaper** as the appetizer, the canapé period. It was the training for what we're doing now. This [*Monocle*] is the magazine I always wanted to do.

Interview
The Chairman

Tyler Brûlé
Editor-in-Chief and
Chairman, *Monocle*

So there was a period of learning 'the corporate', and of learning everything about being a start-up and an SME [small and medium-sized enterprise] as a publisher. By 2005, when we really started thinking seriously about *Monocle*, it was good to kick the tyres and challenge what we wanted to do, so we spoke to private-equity venture-capital firms. They were not interested in magazines, however. We spoke to one or two big publishers to see if they wanted to partner as seed investors, and they said there wasn't a hope, that a magazine like this had no market. But we felt we were on to a good thing; we'd already spoken to advertisers, we had the idea, we had space for it in our building and we could almost hit 'play', but we needed to find investment. We needed the money to get it off the ground.

The wonderful thing was, we had the agency [Winkreative], which could help to do the seed finance [for the magazine], to keep things ticking over. I guess the turning point was a client of the agency who said she loved the idea for the magazine and would like to be one of the early investors, under one condition: that we only brought in other family investors. She said: 'I don't want to sit at a boardroom table with banks or other institutions. I want to sit around a table with people who love magazines and who are real consumers.'

I would say the first lesson in starting a magazine is to choose your partners very carefully. You need investors who are in it for the long haul, not people who are looking to get rich quickly. Also, recognize that we're in a volatile industry. Publishing a magazine will no longer give you the stratospheric rise and then the dip and then the growth. Magazines will flatline for a long time and then gradually grow, but it's unlikely that you'll have the 'rocket start' unless you're a Bauer or a Springer or a Condé Nast and you can throw a lot of money into promoting it. We couldn't – independent publishers just can't do that.

People reading this wouldn't necessarily have the scale of ambition that you had with *Monocle*. Is it possible for a stand-alone indie title to be financially sustainable on sales alone, without being dependent on advertising?
It comes down to what your ambitions are from launch. If you want to produce something beautiful and make a bit of a splash and attract an audience, but also be satisfied that it's going to wash its face or that it's going to lure people into your gallery or get them to commission you to take photographs for them, fine. But to venture forth and launch something and think that it will also set you up and your partner and two kids and a nice house and all those things, without advertising, that's tricky. I can't think of [any] title that is completely contained, free from advertising, [that] really manages to make a profit and sustain itself.

Of course, lots of independent publishers have been in this game before, and don't want the pressure of advertising because they know how complicated and difficult it can be. But I think you have to set your own terms at the beginning. You need to be very clear about how strict the lines are from the very start: will you be willing to blur them at a certain point? Are you willing to cross the line?

2.

1. Tyler Brûlé

2. *Monocle*, issue 1, March 2007

UP
CLOSE
—Global

Preface

It's often the little things that leave a lasting impression when visiting a new city. From flickering neon lights in Portugal to beautifully painted manholes in Japan, Monocle picks out 10 unique and memorable city details.

EDITOR
Tom Morris

 Communal seating in Berlin

From mid-morning onwards in Berlin, the clack-bang of *biergarnitur* tables and benches being unfolded for the day can be heard city-wide. Made from wood and steel, the biertisch (beer table) is the perfect place for a serendipitous meeting – an unshared table is an unthinkable, antisocial decadence. Their design requires a peculiar etiquette: when getting up from sitting on the *bierbank* (beer bench), you must warn those on the end to avoid seesawing. Set out in lines or stacked up for the night, the streets of Berlin fill with these sentinels of outdoor summer life from March to October. —

 Handy doorknockers in Valencia

Vestiges of the Islamic caliphate are dotted all across the Iberian peninsula. In Spain's southern regions some elements have become so heavily integrated into the urban fabric that even locals would struggle to identify their provenance. In the ancient port city of Valencia, hand-shaped doorknockers can still be spotted in the old quarter – remnants of an era when the Moors ruled the land and believed that placing the hand of Fatima on their front doors could ward off evil spirits. Holy Roman Emperor Charles V decreed a ban on Islamic symbols in 1526 but, centuries later, a walk through Valencia's El Carmen district hints at the resilience of these historic hand-me-downs. —

Toronto's unique bike rings

Rolled out during the mid-1980s, these cast-aluminium bicycle-parking rings are now so ubiquitous in Toronto (there are more than 17,000 of them) that they've become the giveaway for residents wherever Toronto plays a stand-in for US metropolises on films and TV. Each ring bears the initials of its creator, local architect David Dennis – then an urban designer for the municipality. Cyclists lock their bikes against the circular shape, which has two contact points for added stability. "By providing secure parking, the rings encourage Torontonians to cycle and reap all its benefits," says Dennis. —

 Drainspotting in Japan

In an age when most pedestrians' eyes are locked on their smartphones, who pays attention to manholes in the street anymore? Be sure to do so in Japan, where more than 10 million of them sit quietly, decorated with colourful illustrations of local birds, trees, landscapes, traditional crafts and more. "It started from a single bureaucrat in the early 1980s," says Noboru Fujiwara at Sewage PR Platform, an expert on the subject. The unknown bureaucrat identified that many people were ashamed they worked in the industry and hoped to change that by using some nice design, Fujiwara explains. The idea encouraged municipal governments and builders to design their manholes without compromising required safety standards. Since then the phenomenon has spread nationwide, from Okinawa to Hokkaido, and has accumulated a collection of 1,800 patterns. —

 Lighting up Lisbon

Neon signage in the Portuguese capital date back to the early years of the Salazar dictatorship where signmaking – like other industrial crafts – was protected by the fascist regime until the 1970s. Their appeal went beyond aesthetics too, as custom neons provide years of round-the-clock, low-cost service. One neighbourhood where they can still be viewed in their original glory is Cais do Sodré, a site where many returning sailors would let loose in the bars (many named after seafaring port cities and nations such as Tokyo, Oslo and Liverpool) and brothels of its sleazy backstreets. Though many old haunts are now being replaced or upgraded, Lisbon nights are still punctuated by this distinctive fluorescent flicker. —

Shop signage in Genoa

Genoa's city centre is dominated by car-free streets where independent retail is still king. Businesses invest in attractive signage with some opting for old-fashioned cursive fonts and others choosing crisper typefaces. Several third-generation firms ply their trade crafting logos on metal, wood and glass, using lettering in gold leaf or embossed in brass. The approach makes shop fronts on the city's historic palazzos look a lot smarter than the backlit plastic signs in favour elsewhere. —

3.

3. *Monocle*, issue 75, July/August 2014, 'City Details' report

4. *Monocle Alpino*, annual large-format newspaper, 2014

5. *Monocle Mediterraneo*, annual large-format newspaper, 2012

Is there much crossover between *Monocle* and Winkreative, in terms of teams and clients?

That goes back to drawing the line. They're two separate companies, both legally on paper and in the way they function. There's surprisingly little crossover. Of course, it happens – I'd like it to happen more, actually. When we started, we thought more of the agency's clients would advertise in the magazine, and that more subjects that we would treat in *Monocle* might become clients of the agency. So it's not as symbiotic as even I would hope, but I think that's also healthy, because *Monocle* stands on its own two feet and has to survive on its own, as does the agency. You could easily uncouple those businesses today and they could continue to thrive and flourish.

How would you assess the health of independent publishing at the moment? How sustainable is the boom?

I think it's a hot question, because from Warsaw to Stockholm to Portland – wherever you want to go in the world – there is a great deal of independent publishing. That's great, and it's wonderful that it's happening, but it faces many challenges; we all do, every day.

We can see that at the mass commercial end, none of the big magazine distributors in this country take a punt on anything. For them, you have to be a sure bet. The specialist outlets are very few and far between. There's a challenge on the horizon: even if people are making enough money, and moving along by selling copies for £10 or £12, there's a distribution wall right now, and that's a massive problem.

I think we're in a period of reaction. There's a surge in all these titles because of the over-digitization of our society. We're seeing this massive reaction with print, self-published print and so on, responding to a wave or onslaught of digital. That will naturally settle down. Whether it's at issue 3 or 6, I think a lot of titles will just fade away, as is always the case. There has been an extraordinary surge in new titles, but I think we'll see a flattening-out.

4.

5.

Can you explain *Monocle*'s rejection of social media platforms like Facebook and Twitter?

People think it's because we're Luddites or whatever, but it's not that – it's purely a business decision and a brand decision. I don't think we always need to be 'on'. Editorially, I think inviting a lot of chat into the conversation dilutes your brand. Yoo, you think you're closer to your audience because you're managing it digitally, but when you invite and create a platform for comment you also create a corner or quadrant for detractors.

The great thing about magazines is that they are contained and considered, and good magazines have a very clear tone. What's wonderful about them is that they exist as a moment in time, and you don't have to add to them. We're very transparent: every single editor's email address is there [in the masthead]. If you don't like something, or if you love it, if you have a comment to make, why don't you just make it to the editor? Why does everything need a platform today?

Then, commercially, it's really simple. A lot of independent publishers have used Twitter to raise awareness about the brand and talk about everything they're doing. The problem with that is that it's largely been the media that has created what Twitter has become. Media companies are finding that advertisers are spending their budgets on Twitter. What you've done [as a publisher] is aided and abetted the competition. My view is, why should I fuel the Twitter machine? I would be the one who helped to bring about my own downfall.

The third element is that sense of demystification. Good magazines are a bit mysterious. Is *Hole & Corner* magazine [produced from] a really nice white studio in Farringdon with beautiful painted beams and just one long table where everyone eats lunch together? I don't know, but that's good. It exists up here [in my head] because that's my vision of that brand. Of course, a lot of these magazines are on social media, but they're not revealing too much. If they do, they denigrate what magazines can do well.

6.

7.

8.

How many copies of *Monocle* do you print? What is the breakdown geographically and between subscriptions and news-stand?

We print about 120,000, and we sell just under 80,000. Pretty much a third goes to North America – the United States is our biggest market, and Canada is our sixth biggest market. Another third goes to Europe, where the two biggest markets are the United Kingdom and Germany. And a third is Asia, led by Australia, Singapore and Hong Kong. Subscriptions tend to make up about 20 per cent of sales. Distribution on news-stand is incredibly important to us.

Is *Monocle* a magazine or is it a brand?

Everyone likes to talk in terms of brands. It's still a magazine – at its core we're nothing without the printed product. It's what makes the money, it's what informs everything else we do. Whatever is on the radio, or whatever is in the shops, or as we develop books, it all starts with what happens month in, month out in the magazine.

If we had to cut everything off and say we're not doing all this other stuff, no cafes, no shops, the magazine would be just fine. We're actually able to do all those other things because of the magazine. The magazine is what finances everything. Yes, retail makes money and the cafe makes money, but we couldn't have started those ventures without the power and the cash flow the magazine generates. So I'm under no illusions as to what *Monocle* is about.

What's the magic of a printed magazine, for you?

I don't want to fashion myself as a press baron, but you realize as you get older that press barons became press barons because they were in the manufacturing business. To me, that's what is exciting about what we do today: there are many moving parts; we're in the business of well and truly making something.

It's interesting when digital colleagues talk about something being 'in beta', and it's going to take I-don't-know-how-long to work the kinks out. But just think, let's go to the north of Finland where they're cutting trees down right now. Those trees are then dragged by snowmobile through the forest, they're put on trucks and trains, they get to the south of Finland, they're put on an icebreaker, they cross the Baltic and then go to a mill in Germany and get turned into paper, which then goes on trucks to England. In the meantime, all these people are being sent around the world [creating content]. Ink and glue and various other components are being purchased. All this comes together and then it all goes down to a printing press in Dorset and it comes out as a finished product. Then the logistics really start and it goes on a Japan Airways freighter to Tokyo and on to a Cathay Pacific freighter to Hong Kong, and on, and on, and out across the world. And you know what? We never miss a deadline.

[If you think of it like that] you see that there are many people in the process and you realize that our sales growth has a direct impact on someone in the north of Finland. For me, the magic is making something physical. You're manufacturing something … In a world that is [becoming] more cloud-based and more desktop-based, that's exciting to me.

9.

Money talks

08

A straight-up and simple guide to planning and running the money side

Neglecting the money side of their project was a common regret among the magazine publishers interviewed for this book. It may not be as much fun as putting together a ten-page feature or organizing your launch event, but financial planning is absolutely essential if you're going to last past issue 1. After you've got to grips with what your magazine's vital stats will be and devised your publishing model, hire a good accountant; as well as doing the practical financial stuff like tax returns and profit and loss statements, they can give you advice on putting together a business plan.

There will always be an element of trial and error in your financial operation, but there are a few steps you can follow and important questions you can ask yourself to make it easier and avoid common pitfalls.

This chapter guides you through the basics of costing, cash flow and funding.

"We had this idea for a magazine, we'd come this far, we had space for it in our building and we could almost hit 'play' and away we go, but we needed to find investment."

Tyler Brûlé, *Monocle*

Costing checklist

Here are the most common costs you have to consider when planning your finances:

✔ Print and paper

✔ Editorial budget: writing, design, proofreading, illustration, photography

✔ Postage and/or fulfilment: sending magazines to individual customers, delivery to warehouse or distributor

✔ Staff wages

✔ Overheads: studio/office, bills

How much money do I need?

Your main financial outlay as a magazine will be the printing and paper costs for each issue. (See Chapter 9 for information on specifying your magazine with a printer.) Depending on how you intend to sell your magazine, you'll need to work out how long it will take you to get revenue from copy sales. (See Chapter 6 on distribution and selling.) You will need enough cash upfront to cover the printing, paper and postage of your first issue, and probably the second issue, too.

The next main cost to consider is creating the content of your magazine. Even the greats like *i-D* started at a kitchen table, printed on a photocopier and stapled by hand. But vivid, well-produced content can beget a classic title. Your editorial budget will depend on what type of magazine you are, and whether you are a one-person enterprise, have an in-house team, or employ freelance contributors for writing, proofreading, photography, illustration and the design of the magazine. Can you do some of these yourself and call in favours, or do you need a budget for all these services and contributors?

Can I make money?

Nobody goes into independent publishing for the money. It is notoriously hard to make money from magazines; even the big

One hand in your pocket: self-funding

LAW

Frequency: Biannual
Date launched: June 2011
Location: London
Cover price: Free
Strapline: 'The youth of today with grit in their teeth and something to say'

LAW magazine came out of John Holt's final-year project as a fashion student at the University of Brighton. Holt made the ultimate sacrifice to fund the launch of his magazine: 'I sold my dream car, a 1974 Ford Escort MK1, and printed 500 copies,' he recalls. The magazine is distributed free in independent boutiques, bookshops, newsagents and record shops around the world. Revenue streams include brand direction and shoot production for fashion brands. At the time of writing, Holt also had other plans in mind: 'We make a bespoke piece of clothing for the cover of each issue, and we are hoping to release some of these pieces in the coming year.'

Perdiz

Frequency: Biannual
Date launched: September 2012
Location: Barcelona
Cover price: €12
Strapline: 'Happiness is contagious'

A shamelessly upbeat and optimistic collection of real-life stories, *Perdiz* is a classic independent publishing venture with a completely personal and non-commercial approach. Yet it sustains a healthy print run of 5,000 copies, and attracts a sponsor for each issue. Its founder, Marta Puigdemasa, funded the launch out of her own pocket: 'Some people spend their savings on houses and cars,' she says; 'I spent them on a mag.' She started the magazine as a way to scratch a creative itch and create her 'dream job': 'Money has never been my goal with *Perdiz*, and maybe that's the reason *Perdiz* is the way it is.'

publishers struggle, often because of outmoded business models. The beauty of indie publishing is that you can, with good planning, make a model to suit you, your means and the way you work.

If you can make your magazine pay for itself you are on to a winner. If you can make it pay you a bit of money for the time you invest in it, that's even better. Most indie magazine-makers work on their publication alongside paid work, but a few do turn their part-time passion into full-time employment. And, of course, there are rare geniuses who turn an independent publishing venture into a profitable global brand. But those often genre-defining titles have serious financial backing from investors, require expert handling and pose considerable risks.

Where to get the cash

About half the magazines interviewed for this book had their launch issue funded by personal savings. The next most popular method was a mixture of investment and loans from friends and family with self-funding and sponsorship.

Sponsorship can take the form of discounts from printers and paper companies. If you can convince them that your product will be a great ambassador for their services and a jewel in their portfolio, they might exchange serious discounts for a small presence in your magazine (like a logo on the masthead page and page adverts).

Crowdsourced funding sites like Kickstarter, Indiegogo and Unbound have helped lots of first-time independent publishers to get their titles off the ground. It has also helped magazines to push forward into their second or third issues. Both the literary magazine *Teller* and the food journal *Put a Egg on It* used crowdfunding to publish their second issues.

Crowdsourcing your funding is basically a way to secure upfront sales, but you can also do that by yourself if you have an online community to tap into, as *Printed Pages* does through its blog, It's Nice That. It means you have the cash in the bank to pay for production, making each issue less of a financial risk.

The ultimate form of upfront funding for magazines is subscriptions (see chapter 6), but it can be difficult to win people's trust to invest in future issues unless your magazine is very clearly built on a 'must-read' editorial concept. *Delayed Gratification* attracted a good subscriptions base early through its 'slow journalism' concept, making readers feel that they simply must not miss each quarterly instalment.

It is a tall order to secure funding through advertising for the first issue of a magazine. In reality you need at least one issue to show to potential advertisers, and a good indication of the number of readers you are reaching before they will be convinced to pay for a presence in your title.

Revenue streams

There are many ways that your project can make money. Finding the right combination of revenue streams is a matter of thinking carefully about your publishing model and playing to your strengths.

▶ **Copy sales** The most obvious way to generate revenue from magazines is through copy sales. You can do a combination of selling direct to readers, through retailers and via distribution companies (see chapter 6).

▶ **Subscriptions** The most reliable and profitable way to sell copies is through subscriptions, but that comes with its own set of considerations (see pages 100–101).

▶ **Advertising/advertorials** Not all magazines can rely on advertising sales for funding, but approached in the right way it can be a very productive part of your model (see chapter 7).

▶ **Events** Joining in with existing events is important for promoting your sales, but you might also run your own. With an audience that is large and properly engaged you can generate revenue through ticket sales.

▶ **Products/merchandise** If you have an eager audience regularly parting with money for copies of your magazine, you could expand your product range (see page 156).

Self-sufficiency versus sponsorship

Boat

Frequency: Biannual
Date launched: Spring 2011
Print run: 7,000
Cover price: £8
Number of full-time staff: One

The makers of *Boat* approach its funding issue-by-issue, self-financing the production of each edition and then recouping the cost through revenue generated by advertising and copy sales. 'It's more of a risk to do it this way,' says its founding editor, Erin Spens, 'because not every issue has recouped the money we put into it.' She is passionate about transparency in the relationship between editorial and advertising. 'Our model means we can say 100 per cent what you read in *Boat* is what we found or what a local wanted to say, rather than what a brand wants us to talk about.' *Boat*'s print run has grown steadily from 1,500 copies at its launch to 7,000 at issue 8.

Colors

Frequency: Biannual
Date launched: 1991
Print run: 20,000
Cover price: €13
Number of full-time staff:
Eight to ten

Colors was launched by Oliviero Toscani and Tibor Kalman in the early 1990s and instantly became a benchmark for its iconoclastic editorial and design. Its current editor-in-chief, Patrick Waterhouse, has worked on *Colors* since 2011. It is produced from the Fabrica research centre in Treviso, Italy, which is financed by the Benetton Group. Arguably not strictly 'independent' because of its funded status, *Colors* nonetheless has a sense of freedom in common with indie titles. 'It has its own issues and some of the same problems in terms of distribution, but it is in the privileged position of having a sponsor,' says Waterhouse. 'You can have independent-minded thinking with proper funding. It is a very fortunate situation.'

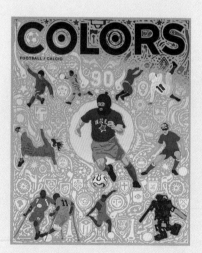

Funding buffet: find cash where you can

Vestoj

Frequency: Annual
Date launched: 2009
Print run: 3,000
Cover price: €15

Formerly editor of *Acne Paper*, Anja Aronowsky Cronberg dealt with her frustration over fashion publishing by launching her own title. 'We're not news-based, we have no advertising and we don't urge our contributors to use or refer to any particular brands ... we look at fashion as a mirror [of], and a way to understand, our culture,' she says. Before launching, she worked hard at fundraising, securing sponsorship from a printer, binder and paper supplier. *Vestoj* is poised between fashion academia and the fashion industry. 'We are now published by London College of Fashion,' she reveals, 'so our revenue is a combination of the budget LCF supplies and what we make on sales.'

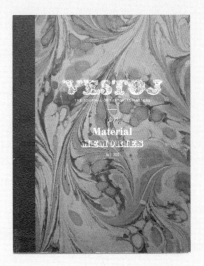

Teller

Frequency: Irregular
Date launched: 2010
Print run: 1,000
Cover price: £7

'A magazine of stories,' *Teller* includes fiction, reportage, photostories, graphic art 'and anything else we can find that we feel tells a really good story', say its makers, Katherine Hunt and Ruby Russell. They funded the first issue themselves and used Kickstarter to crowdfund the second. Asked what their biggest publishing mistake has been, they admit to having priced their first issue too low. 'It's difficult to make it work financially,' they say, 'but there is a lot of support and enthusiasm out there – from customers, bookshops, other interested parties, people with stories to tell – for independent publications.'

A sample projection

There are almost as many different publishing models as there are magazines (see chapter 2), but as a basic demonstration, here is a fictional projection on an issue-by-issue basis, highlighting some things to consider.

Let's say you are planning a biannual magazine, produced in your spare time:
You print 2,000 copies of issue 1. The cover price is £10.
You allocate 1,000 copies to a distributor; 980 to sell online; and 20 to send as promotional copies.

Costs		Revenue	
£5,000	You pay £2.50 a copy for **print**, **paper**, **binding** and **delivery** of 2,000 copies.	**£5,000**	**Month 1** You sell 500 copies online in the first month (and include a postage charge on top of the cost of the magazine).
£1,000	You pay someone you know to do the **design**.	**£3,400**	**Month 4** Based on a dummy you made with the printer and PDFs from the designer, you have a deal with a distributor that will take 1,000 copies.
£0	You call in favours from freelance **writers**, **photographers** and **illustrators**.		According to the terms of the contract, you will get a quarterly sales report and invoice for copies sold on 30-day terms.
£0	You edit it from your kitchen table, so there are no office or staff **overheads**.		That means that you will be paid about four months after supplying the magazines.
£40	You post out 20 **promotional copies** to press and other contacts in the United Kingdom and Europe.		The distributor's terms state that you will receive 40 per cent revenue from sold copies (£4 per copy).
£50	You make a **website** from a customized WordPress template and pay £100 annual hosting fees (or £50 per issue).		During the first three months the distributor's retailers sell 850 copies of the magazine. The distributor pays you £3,400.
£120	The website uses PayPal for **online sales**, which means £20 per month PayPal merchant fees (£240 per year, or £120 per issue).	**£4,800**	**Month 6** You sell out of the other 480 copies over the next five months.
£500	You hold a **launch event** at a friend's venue.		
£6,710 Total cost of the issue		**£13,200 Total revenue from the issue** (over 6 months)	

That's a profit of £6,490

Well done – that's almost enough to cover the costs for issue 2, if you cut back a little or put in the shortfall yourself. Now see the opposite page for some tweaks and fixes to maximize your margins and efficiency.

A few magazines surveyed for this book received funding from public bodies and educational institutions in the form of grants and bursaries. If you and your title have links to education or can make a legitimate application to bodies like Arts Council England, this is a fantastically advantageous route not only to funding but also to credibility.

Killer cash flow

Cash flow, or rather the inability to plan your cash flow, can be crippling. Unless you're a natural with figures, or have the time to teach yourself what you need to know, you'll bless the day you hired a good accountant.

You might calculate that the first issue of your magazine will make £13,000 revenue (see the example projection opposite), but when will you collect that money? Can you predict how long it will take you to sell the copies you have allocated to online sales through your website? What is the agreement with your distributor: will you have to wait 120 days for your money, or longer? If you are managing distribution yourself, remember that you might have to do a lot of nagging to individual retailers for lots of small sums of money in order to get paid. What payment terms are your advertisers on?

The revenue from your first issue could take several months to hit your bank account, and meanwhile there might be bills to pay. Check whether the revenue from issue 1 will reach you before you have to start paying costs like print and paper for issue 2. Don't get caught in the red before you have even put out your second issue, and if you do foresee a deficit, make sure you have a prearranged overdraft or loan in place from your bank or elsewhere.

Learn how to make regular, simple profit and loss (known as P&L) statements, or ask your accountant to prepare one. A P&L is a snapshot of the current state of your finances during a specific period of time, showing your revenue and your expenses. It will show you if you are making any money (or not), and help you to work out where you need to make changes to your expenditure. Templates for a basic P&L are available on easily accessible apps, accounting software and online, but getting a decent accountant and asking them to help you with your P&L will be money well spent if you don't have a head for figures.

Projections like the one opposite can help you to decide your cover price. Is it high enough to cover costs? You can either increase the price or reduce costs.

Tweaks and fixes

What can you do with the next issue to increase your margins and put yourself in a position to grow? These are your options:

▶ **Allocate more copies to sell online,** as that's more profitable and the money reaches you more quickly. Think about how you would promote these sales, and remember that it will mean extra work for you.

▶ **Talk to your distributor.** Where did you sell out, and where were copies left? Can you improve efficiency and thus revenue?

▶ **Try to sell a few pages of advertising,** using issue 1 as a sales tool.

▶ **Reduce your costs** by approaching printers and paper companies for sponsorship.

▶ **Alternatively, streamline the product.** Talk to your designer and printer about a cheaper paper or binding method, but be careful to get the balance right: always maintain a level of quality that justifies your cover price.

▶ **Get involved in events,** and attempt to create opportunities to promote and sell your magazine directly to readers.

1.

Interview
The Printer

Mark Shields
Printer
CPI Colour and Park Communications

Finding the right printer to work with can make all the difference in running a tight ship and producing a top-quality printed object – critical ingredients in any independent publishing venture. Mark Shields of London print company CPI Colour (interviewed here during his time at Park Communications) offers tips and trade secrets to help you find print perfection.

How can a good printer help an independent publishing client?

Your printer must give you good advice and be able to say 'You can do that, but maybe in a different way and a cost-effective way.' That's the way we worked at Park and at CPI Colour. We're able to advise [our clients] and recommend changes that will save money but still achieve the desired look and effects.

Which indie magazines do you print?

We do *Riposte*, *Disegno*, *Printed Pages*, *Protein*, *Wrap*, *Rosie Magazine*, YCN's *You Can Now* – about eight to ten titles, as well as other magazines and other literature.

How did your relationships with the indie magazine world come about?

Through a recommendation to speak to It's Nice That, *Printed Pages* came in, and it went from there. It's taken us into a different area. Working on *Printed Pages* was quite exciting because they had a vision for where they wanted to take the magazine. They had a set budget [for] between five and eight thousand copies, so we helped them come up with a way to do it.

So the right relationship with a printer is crucial?

It's one of the most important things. We have become involved in *Printed Pages*' Here seminars and the Nicer Tuesdays events [in London]. A lot of people [come] up to me who are looking to produce magazines – anything from 100 up to 25,000 copies. [We are] in the marketplace because of our knowledge and track record, and because people see what *Printed Pages* is about and how it looks and feels. It really has taken us into a different market.

What are the key considerations for someone starting from scratch who knows virtually nothing about printing? How should they think about print when planning a mag?

I would write a simple list: the cover, how many pages, has it got a flap on it, two flaps? Number of pages of text, the kind of paper you're looking for: coated, uncoated or glossy, is it thin, has it got a flex to it, is it floppy, is it thicker? With just that information, your printer can understand what it is you're looking for. Also, if there's a reference point such as a magazine you like, a printer can quote for something based on it.

Break it up into bite-sized pieces that are understandable as a little list – '500 copies, 4-page cover, 150 pages of text, four-colour process throughout, cover needs to be really glossy

1. Mark Shields, portrait by Ivan Jones

2. Publications printed by Mark Shields

2.

and the logo picked out in some shape or form, mix of papers, square-backed or saddle-stitched' – and that's enough to start the ball rolling on getting some costs together.

Could you explain the difference between litho and digital printing?

Digital is very economical for something that's up to about 60–100 pages at a low print run. Once you get to over 25 to 50 copies at that size, litho tends to be more economical. There's a threshold, so it's always worth looking at both options before you commit. The turnaround with digital is really quick, but you're limited as to papers and finishes … It can be a little less versatile.

3.

What is the process at your end, starting from the point at which you receive artwork from the publisher?

When we get the artwork we do a pre-flight check to see if all is OK. We will highlight any low-resolution images that don't look good, check the bleed, make sure there are no missing fonts, make sure double-page spreads line up, and [point out] other artworking issues. Sometimes we prefer to have open files [e.g. Adobe InDesign files] rather than PDFs, because then we can change the way the artwork is set up to print, to achieve the best results.

Then we'll send the client the magazine proof, which can be a PDF or physical proof. PDFs are checked on screen; physical proofs are coated or uncoated inkjet paper proofs, calibrated to our presses. We can produce a set of proofs in about 24 hours from receiving the artwork. The client signs them off, then – depending on the format – the average job takes five to seven working days, whether it's two or three thousand copies or 50,000 copies.

What are the mechanics? Who are the people involved in the process on the factory floor?

I lead the project, and an account manager is assigned to our client for the day-to-day running. He or she will process the various things within the production that need to be ordered and organized, such as inks and paper, and any special artworking processes, such as foil blocking, debossing, UV varnishing. The production team then organizes the printing on one of our three presses, along with the finishing and any other processes involved. The magazine starts by going into the studio, where an operator will take responsibility for the job, imposing the pages into sections so that when printed and folded they are all in the correct order. Any other artwork problems can also be sorted at this time. Once the operator has planned the job and made a final check, he will put it into the output device – an Epson proofer – which runs out the proofs.

Once the job is signed off by the client, it comes back to the account manager, who will organize any final corrections. Corrected pages are proofed back to the client via PDF, and when those are signed off the studio will make the printing plates. These go out to the machine room, where the job is printed.

3. Printed matter on the shelves at CPI Colour, Clerkenwell, London

4. Publications printed by Mark Shields

On the printing press, one machine minder plus an assistant run the job. Depending on the pagination and print run, the magazine may take one or more shifts to complete. When the printed sheets are dry, one or more folding machines will fold the text pages. The cover will be laminated or have any other finishes applied to it. The collated text and cover are then bound on the binding machine, either saddle-stitched, perfect-bound, PUR-bound or thread-sewn.

Are there any common pitfalls people can avoid?
You've got to remember to talk to your printer. Make sure you remember things like allowing bleed on images, and converting files to CMYK. With solid colours, you should try to underpin blacks with a cyan, but we'll pick that [sort of thing] up. What I always ask for is that people send over the latest file when it's in progress. That way, I can check it and pick up on anything – it could even be something like the wrong number of pages. I always advise people to make a little dummy themselves by running the pages out on their printer and folding them up. It always needs to be in multiples of 8 or 16. When you're designing your book, you want it to be divisible by those – ideally 16, because most printers will be working in 16s. To have an odd 4 or 8 is more expensive, and a whole load of paper will be wasted. Also, printers won't necessarily be setting up for 8 and 4, so they'd have to re-set up a folding machine to do that, which will probably cost you more money.

Are there also efficiencies in size and format that people should bear in mind?
Yes. Working in the A-formats is successful, likewise slightly over or under. Talk to your printer, because there might be certain slightly bigger or smaller sizes that would work better. That maximizes what you get out of each sheet without wastage.

Do you observe a change in the way people are making magazines?
Yes, very much so. They are putting more creativity into them, they're not just making a straightforward cover-and-80-pages-of-text … some of the magazines we get involved with have that special something about them that gives the reader that little bit extra.

4.

People are using mixtures of papers, different finishes, short pages within the text, 8-page and 6-page covers, all sorts of things. Mixed papers are a big trend. Also, short-sectioned mixed papers: a magazine made from all coated or uncoated paper, but with a different section, maybe A5 within an A4 or a short-cut section. Coated, highly glossy papers are coming back in vogue, with varnish on them. The textured cover paper is a major thing.

Once you've got the essence of the idea, you can do things in a different way. You don't have to spend lots of money on materials, but you can do things to achieve tactile finishes and visual effects that enhance the final product.

Launch and beyond

09

Going to print

Finding your audience
and building a
readership

Promoting your title

Finding a smooth route to market

It's time to turn all the ideas and hard graft into a physical reality, send that magazine off to print and connect with some readers. Try to strike a balance between keeping the momentum going and rushing something through. It's worth taking the time to get your launch issue right, but resist endlessly tweaking and fiddling. There comes a point when you must take the plunge and show the world what you're made of.

'I just did it,' recalls Cathy Olmedillas of *Anorak*. 'The first issue was launched. I sent out a press release that made this really great big fuss about it. H&M saw that press release, so did Borders, and that press release got me started – H&M supported it from issue 1, which was incredible. Borders took an order as well. So then it was a reality.'

This chapter will guide you through the process of printing and promoting your launch issue. But that second issue will soon come around, so get used to putting some pressure on yourself to deliver to a deadline. For a quarterly title, you might have spent a year or more finely crafting your launch issue, but then you'll have just three months until the readers you've so painstakingly enticed will be expecting the next one.

Going to print

Finding a friendly, helpful printer will make a huge difference to your experience of publishing a magazine, particularly at the start of your voyage into independent publishing, when the terminology and the processes of print might be new and intimidating. Kai Brach, publisher of *Offscreen*, is based in Australia but prints his magazine in his native Germany, where printing is cheaper and where it is also cheaper to send copies on around the world. 'They held my hand,' he says of his printer, 'and guided me through the process of first going to print.'

To find your printer, ask around and look at which firms are used by other independent magazines. Meet potential printers in person – it's important to work with a printer you get on with, and who understands your product.

For independent publishers, the quality of their magazine as an object is crucial to the way it is received. For many art directors and publishers, this means working with a printer who is willing to go the extra mile and who understands the need for precision, accuracy and special processes. 'We always go on press for the cover,' says Veronica Ditting of *The Gentlewoman*. 'We don't use normal Pantone colours … Never let the detail go, even at the final stage.'

When you've found some printers you'd like to work with, specify what you want and get some quotations.

1.

1. Issue 9 of *Offscreen* on press

A basic specification should include:

Size: the dimensions of the magazine. Printers will advise on the most economical sizes that can be got out of a sheet of paper.

Number of pages: the most economical numbers are divisible into full 'signatures', or sections of 16 pages, but you can also add sections of 8 and 4 pages.

Cover pages: usually these consist of a front cover, inside front cover, inside back cover and outside back cover. You would express a 112-page magazine with a typical 4-page cover like this as '112 pages +4'.

Type and weight of paper: either a specific paper stock or a choice between coated and uncoated. Weight is expressed in 'gsm', meaning 'grams per square metre'. Your printer can advise on your options, and you can request samples from paper companies.

Finishing: including foil blocking, embossing, varnishing or special colours.

Binding: such as perfect-bound, PUR-bound, saddle-stitched, sewn or casebound.

Quantity: the number of copies to be printed.

Delivery: where you want copies sent, and the quantities. This might include editorial copies and copies destined for a distributor or fulfilment house.

2. *Riposte*, issue 4, 2015, spread showing bound-in short page section

Pre-print checklist

This handy checklist from Mark Shields of CPI Colour gives common pitfalls to be aware of before sending your job to print:

✔ Make sure that trim marks are set up correctly.

✔ There should be a minimum 3 mm bleed on trim edges.

✔ Check that CMYK conversions are done correctly.

✔ Any special colours must be set up properly.

✔ For the best colour results, use a resolution of 300 dpi.

✔ Check how your printer requires the pages to be supplied. Single pages are normally best.

Spot the difference: tight cover concepts

The Gentlewoman

Frequency: Biannual
Date launched: 2010
Location: London
Cover price: £6
Strapline: 'Fabulous women's magazine'

Twice a year there is great excitement among *The Gentlewoman*'s readers: who will be the magazine's newest cover star? It is a powerful tool for the title, not only creating a sense of anticipation, but also compounding each time the visual style and editorial attitude that sets it so far apart from other women's fashion magazines. A sense of occasion surrounds each launch, which is celebrated with a readers' club event. *The Gentlewoman* has grown steadily since its first issue both in physical size (from 178 to 296 pages) and in print run (from 72,000 copies at issue 1 to 89,000 by issue 10).

Put a Egg on It

Frequency: Biannual
Date launched: 2008
Location: New York City
Cover Price: $7
Strapline: 'Tasty Zine!'

Put a Egg on It is a delicious earworm of a title. 'It's a thing we always say to each other. If you're out for dinner and there's even a little bit left over, you're like "Hey, I'll take it home and put a egg on it!"' say the food magazine's makers, Sarah Keough and Ralph McGinnis. The founders lead the Little Magazine Coalition, a support network for local indie publishers. As well as meeting to share experiences and advice, the group attempts to tackle the financial and logistical problems facing indie titles, with initiatives such as negotiating a group discount with a printer.

3.

3. *Frank*, newsprint publication for UK illustration agency Handsome Frank, printed by Newspaper Club

4. IndieCon 2015 visual identity

5. IndieCon delegates peruse publications and an exhibition by independent publishers at IndieCon 2015

Defining your print run

How many copies of your first issue should you print? Getting the numbers right for the first order can be tricky. Selling out is good, but you don't want to underestimate your potential.

If you don't have much money upfront, there is no harm in starting small. Using an on-demand device like Newspaper Club to make a modest newsprint edition that you send to key people and sell online alongside your blog content is a cheap way to get your name out there and begin to attract a readership.

Cereal magazine started small, printing 1,500 copies of volume 1 in December 2012, but by December 2014 it had grown to the point of selling 25,000 copies worldwide. 'We made a huge list of shops around the world that I really wanted to be in, and I just started calling them,' explains Rosa Park. 'We ended up selling all 1,500 copies within our first month, so I printed another 1,500.'

Consulting a distributor and key retailers can help you to decide your initial print run. Treat issue 1 as a pilot, test the response and build on it.

> ## "Don't ask yourself too many questions. Act fast on ideas and see what happens."
>
> **Olivier Talbot,** *Acid*

Publicity and community

Aim to sell as many copies as possible when you first launch an issue, since the noise you can create on social media and in the press is likely to diminish as the launch story fades. When Kai Brach launches an issue of *Offscreen*, he sells 500–1,000 copies of his 4,000-copy print run in the first week.

Use every tool you have to promote a new issue. Social media can drive traffic to your online shop, but Will Hudson of INT Works and *Printed Pages* believes that nothing beats a newsletter: 'No matter the power of social media, a newsletter is where we get spikes in sales,' he says. 'It's amazing how you can tweet about something, you can Facebook it, but the minute you put something in people's inboxes saying "This has launched, click here to buy it now," that's when you still see the highest traction.'

See more on social media on page 81

Building a readership steadily is your goal, and you should aim to increase your print run every few issues. As an independent publisher, you don't have the power of numbers on your side, so promote your magazine in a targeted way, and make every copy and piece of coverage count. Make friends in your industry, its associated press and the indie publishing world, attend events and trade shows, and try to get speaking gigs at events and conferences. Enter awards and blow your own trumpet. Send out press releases when your new issue comes out, and tailor them to highlight specific aspects of your content that might appeal to individual press partners.

See the Little black book section on pages 158–61 for a list of societies, events and awards

'Community is incredibly important,' says the editor of *Boat*, Erin Spens, 'from logistical questions, recommending shipping companies or how to get something through customs, all the way down to promoting your launch party. When there are so many indie mags around you, you think 'We can do this – and not have to rely on advertising Cartier watches to do it.'

4.

5.

1.

Interview
The Innovator

Peter Bil'ak
Founder and Editor,
Works That Work

Dutch designer Peter Bil'ak's *Works That Work* has become an experiment in redesigning the independent publishing model. Bil'ak has applied his designer's brain to every part of the process, from format to advertising to distribution, devising revolutionary systems along the way. Here, he talks in depth about the process, and offers inspiring and practical ideas for anyone interested in the workings of magazine-making.

Have you redesigned the independent publishing model with *Works That Work*?

I think I would describe us as a 'dependent' magazine, not an 'independent' magazine, because we are fully dependent on our readers – we only exist if there are readers who are willing to support us.

Publishing gets interesting once you look beyond what is visible, because people always talk about the layout and the level of writing and photography, and rarely look at what allows them to make it happen. So *Works That Work* became an exercise in looking at all the invisible parts of running a magazine, from financing to distribution, production – all parts that are usually behind the scenes.

Today people are interested in looking at how restaurants operate and how chefs cook and how sports teams train. In the same way, it's nice to get people involved in showing what's underneath the surface of a magazine.

You are very transparent about how *Works That Work* operates. Why is that important to you?

We do it for the readers. That's the simplest starting point, which may sound obvious, but if you consider the traditional magazine [model] it may be radical as well. Most magazines are not made for readers, they are made for advertisers. The revenue comes from advertising, not from subscriptions. For the majority of magazines, readers contribute a really small proportion of the revenue streams. If you look at a magazine's pages, 54 per cent ads is the industry average. But financially, ads contribute up to 90–98 per cent, so a really tiny proportion comes from readers. And therefore, the obligation is not to the readers but to the advertisers. The readership basically becomes a commodity that is sold to the advertisers.

If you reverse it, and say you want to make a magazine for the readers, it has consequences on many different levels ... starting from distribution, because distribution is set up around the model of magazines being made for advertisers. Unsold issues are destroyed because they don't really have a value. They cannot be resold. So you have to rethink the distribution.

You have to consider things that have been taken for granted for a long time because it has been a very successful model and the model of the advertiser-financing is two centuries old. It works for some mags but not others. It's a good time to really look at alternatives.

1. Peter Bil'ak, photograph by Ivan Jones

2.

You have pioneered a system of 'social distribution' with *Works That Work* whereby readers buy magazines at 50 per cent of the cover price and sell them on to retailers or individuals. Is it successful?

It is. When we were starting, it was just a proposal, and it was very hard to make any assumptions about how it might work. It was clear that we had to do something about distribution, as working with a traditional distributor was not really an option. Selling magazines online is great because of course you get full revenue, but it's limiting in that it stays within a group of people who know the magazine. It does not get to the wider public.

Our magazine is designed for the wider public, it is a design magazine for non-designers. But most of the people who come to our website are designers; the people who are most loyal are designers. We're interested in their friends too, the biggest group of people, [but] it's really tricky to get there. This [social distribution] was an attempt to get outside the circle.

The way we approach articles is to make everything very accessible. People from any profession could be interested in the magazine, and we always say it's not made for a particular target group. Social distribution may not be financially the most rewarding [method], but it really enlarges the circle. People appreciate that it works well with the spirit of the magazine – we look at the logistics, we make the invisible visible. By talking about it, people understand why this magazine operates in this particular way.

Do you think it taps into why people love magazines – feeling part of something – and takes it to the next level?

Absolutely. And practically, it has worked better than I expected. With our new way of distributing, we have sold magazines in South America, India, Russia, in distant Asia. These are the markets we would otherwise never be able to access.

With my previous magazine *Dot Dot Dot* we never sold anything in Lebanon or Dubai or Santiago de Chile. But now, suddenly, we are getting plenty of interest from these places. Because of social distribution, people have seen the magazine and ask for it again. So we organize more events there – with our readers' help – and we create a kind of community.

How did you come up with the idea of asking people to take magazines in their luggage to reach other readers and retailers?

It was simple. I travel a lot myself, and I realized that if I go for a two-day trip I would probably take a very small suitcase, and I could check more in. I thought there might be people in the same situation, going places and with free space in their suitcase. Shipping was the most significant cost that we had as a magazine – to get a small stack of magazines to the United States cost as much as the magazines themselves, so it doubled the price. Often, the magazine became too expensive

2. *Works That Work*, issue 1, Winter 2013

3. *Works That Work*, issue 4, 2014, article on South Sudan's state symbols

to [make it worth bothering]. This became a spontaneous way to cut costs and save on shipping through people volunteering to use their luggage space. No one is doing it for money, it is a voluntary, unpaid service – people just want to do it. Now we have a section of the website where people can plan their trips and organize taking magazines from place to place. Often now it happens without my assistance.

Is *Works That Work* breaking even and paying for itself?

It's breaking even, but it's still early days. We've had three issues out, so it's only been a year and a half and, based on previous experience, I know it's too early to come to any conclusions. It could go any way. But we're going to print a bit more of the next issue, and printing more and selling more means that we pay all the contributors and collaborators. We want to make sure that everyone gets paid. I'm the last in the chain. I haven't been paid yet. I would love to be paid for my work, but I'm not in a rush because I'm in the very fortunate position that my income comes from different projects – I have a design studio, so the other 50 per cent of my time is something that makes my living. Ultimately, though, I would love to have designed a project with *Works That Work* that gives everyone their share and is a living thing on its own.

BRANDING THE WORLD'S NEWEST COUNTRY

Top: Declaring his identity as a citizen of a new nation, a man celebrates the birth of South Sudan with its flag painted on his face. Photo: Paul Banks, United Nations

Right: South Sudanese children rehearse a dance routine to be performed at half-time during South Sudan's national football team's match with Kenya as part of the Independence Day celebrations. Photo: Paul Banks, United Nations

South Sudan's Independence Day was set for only six months after the referendum that established the new country's independence from Sudan. In that short time state symbols had to be proposed, refined, adopted and promulgated to a country still torn by internal conflict.

3.

Kwikpoint guides enable basic communication between US troops and locals in Afghanistan and Iraq. Each one requires careful research to determine what things may need to be said, and how to communicate them across barriers of language and culture.

The Afghans were not offended by the cartoonish depictions of bomb detonations, hidden Improvised Explosive Devices (IEDs), or hostage situations. No, the illustration choice that they rejected was the flesh-toned skin of the medical diagram's human form. 'It was considered pornographic,' says Alan Stillman, founder and CEO of the visual communications company Kwikpoint. 'People wouldn't use it and didn't like it because they're so religious there.'

At first glance, the androgynous medical illustration, along with miniaturised drawings of IEDs, turban-topped bomb-makers, and soldiers alternately inquisitive and distressed, could be mistaken for yet another piece of dark comedic satire à la *South Park* or *Family Guy*. But these cartoons are not cynicism-wracked bits of entertainment. Rather, they constitute unique graphic tools available to US armed forces on the battlefield: Kwikpoint's Visual Language Translators.

Approximately the size and shape of a fold-out road map, the guide's laminated panels contain a series of thematically grouped pictograms enabling communication between soldiers and 'native locals'. Need medical attention? Point to an ambulance. Need to know where the guns are stashed? Point to the picture of a weapons cache. The icons symbolise everything from modes of transportation (car, van, bus, bicycle, camel, etc.) to complex concepts relating to transactions and health (I'll reward you for telling me where to find a downed helicopter; show me where it hurts), all at the tip of a soldier's finger.

The Kwikpoint guides occupy a strange space in the world of 2D images, not quite info-graphics but certainly more than mere illustration. Visual Communications Director Stephanie Stierhoff says that working on the pictograms is not dissimilar to working on the icons and logos she designed during a stint on Madison Avenue. Both require simple forms and distinguishing features. Both are distillations of a larger idea. Both aim to achieve immediate viewer recognition. And yet, as she says, making the guides is different from making any other kind of product.

'This affects people directly,' Stierhoff tells me. 'When people go out in the field, they're using our guides for very critical ideas, whether it be a user guide to put on a ballistic vest correctly or communicating ideas to a local in Afghanistan. If we don't do our research, and don't convey these ideas precisely, as precisely as we can possibly do it, it could really have an effect on that person.'

Hence the research. And the necessity to address the pornographic implications of their flesh-coloured medical image. After a bit more experimentation, the Kwikpoint design team changed the flesh colour to a cyanotic robin's-egg blue, transforming a pornographic human figure into an abstract one. 'People look at it and kind of laugh and go, "Well, are you looking for aliens?" or "Do they have blue people there?"' relates Kwikpoint's founder Alan Stillman. He continues, 'And we say, no, this is just a cultural adjustment we have to make.'

Stillman, a maths whizz who got into Cornell's mathematics programme at the age of 16, didn't begin his career with the dream of creating military translators and IED identification guides. Rather, the idea was sown along a 15,000-mile international bike journey he took in the late 1980s. Outside Hungary, Stillman and a friend clipped pictures out of magazines to illustrate a few basic needs, the idea being that if all else failed, they could implore someone for help by pointing to what they wanted.

After Stillman returned to the States in 1988, the idea of making a picture-dictionary continued to pull at his thoughts. The concept was simple yet effective: a collection of pictograms that could be pointed at to communicate the things a traveller might need. Finally, in 1989, after fail-

Barbara Eldredge, who writes on design from New York, interviewed a number of US war veterans about their experience with the visual translator guides.

POINT ME
WHERE IT HURTS

Top: Around five million of Kwikpoint's guides and cards have been issued to military personnel. The laminated, pocket-sized pamphlets are handier and more durable than conventional printed dictionaries and manuals. Above, a US soldier in Afghanistan communicates with a local elder using one of the Kwikpoint Visual Language Translators. Photo courtesy of Kwikpoint.

4.

How does your custom-built subscription software work?
I subscribe to a few magazines and I'm always surprised at how strange the experience is: you make a financial commitment but it becomes something you cannot control. I felt that subscriptions should start and end at any point, as you desire. If I no longer want to get a magazine, I should be able to say so. I made a small survey and most people agreed. So we have a continuous subs that you can turn on or off at any point. And if you want to pause, it's paused. That has to do with the fact that we built a custom payment system … when the new issue is out we charge people's cards and send them the issue, rather than controlling the expiry dates of the subscription. People can start it or stop it with a single email or by logging in to the website. That's how I would want to buy a subscription.

Is this something that could be an app available to other indie publishers?
That was something I thought about, because I'm used to building tools. My main source of income is typography and building fonts; the fonts are the final product, but often we're making tools to create fonts. For example, we created special software to make Arabic fonts, because it didn't exist on Macintosh. We license these tools and it helps to repay the development costs.

ULTIMATE
BACKUP

5.

One building in Hong Kong houses a diverse international community that has a major impact on trade all over Africa and Asia.

CHUNGKING MANSIONS
—
THE WORLD INSIDE THE BUILDING

Chungking Mansions is a dilapidated 17-storey building at the heart of Hong Kong's tourist district. Thousands of people of any of the 129 different nationalities recorded in the guesthouse logs stay in the guesthouses on any given night. The building's already dodgy reputation was immortalised in Wong Kar-wai's 1994 movie Chungking Express.

While to an outsider the building may seem a dangerous ghetto, for the insider it is a hive of prosperity. Here one can find Pakistani merchants, African buyers, American hippies, Hindus, Sikhs, Muslims; tiny hotel rooms, money-changing stalls, curry stands, internet cafés, a snack bars, barber shops, laundries, computer repair services, prostitutes, stores selling mobile phones, clothing, shoes and watches; a constantly changing kaleidoscope of business and cultural interchange. Perhaps the only thing that seems to be lacking is native Hong Kongers.

Anthropologist Gordon Mathews started researching the building in 2006, staying in all 96 of its guesthouses, spending every available moment there in an effort to answer questions like 'What has brought all these different people here?' and 'Who lives this place into?' His research culminated in his book Ghetto at the Centre of the World. Peter Bialo spoke to Mathews about how the Chungking Mansions traders do business and why they carry their goods to their own homes instead of shopping them in containers: in short, about how most of the world experiences globalisation today.

Gordon Mathews is a professor of anthropology at the Chinese University of Hong Kong, teaching Meanings of Life, amongst other subjects. He spends his free time hanging out at Chungking Mansions.

Paul Hilton usually photographs wildlife, but for this assignment he returned to Chungking Mansions, where he had stayed when on his first trip to Hong Kong.

6.

Originally, the plan was to license the publishing tools to magazines, but it's slightly more complicated because I realized that to make it work for ourselves is a lot easier than to make a general tool for everyone: the workflows are so different [on different magazines]. For example, people work with a different payment system, or their country doesn't allow them to do recurring payments, and suddenly it stops working. To solve it properly would be a project on its own, so, although I'm not against sharing these tools or allowing other people to use them, it's not as straightforward as I thought. To make a real product would take another year of work, which I don't have time to invest.

We launched with crowdfunding for the first issue, but instead of going to Kickstarter or some existing platform, we created our own crowdfunding platform. It was a bit of a gamble, but we needed to solve the problem of the payment platform to continue running the magazine … I don't know if I would recommend that others do it that way – it was quite an expensive way to start.

What questions should aspiring magazine publishers ask themselves?

The motivation for making the magazine should be clear, and the motivation is something that should not change. They should always come back to it and say 'If my intention is clear, does this issue live up to my intentions?'

Make it very personal. I'm doing *Works That Work* because I'm learning a lot of stuff along the way … it keeps bringing up things that I don't know anything about.

What's the most important thing you've learned about indie publishing?

I knew – but had forgotten – that launching something is easier than keeping it, maintaining it and running it in the long term. I think the common mistake is that all the energy goes into the launch, and launches usually go right because people love new things.

But for me, I think the most important issue was that second issue, because then you have to confirm it and you have to show that you can keep up the level and get better.

4. *Works That Work*, issue 1, Winter 2013, article on Kwikpoint guides

5. *Works That Work*, issue 3, 2014, article on Norway's Global Seed Vault, photography by Cary Fowler

6. *Works That Work*, issue 2, 2013, article on Hong Kong's Chungking Mansions, photography by Paul Hilton

10

Growing up

From part-time project
to self-sustaining
business

Do new stuff

Take stock and
celebrate

How fledgling magazines go from simply surviving to spreading their wings

In your first year or two, it will be an achievement just to be making enough sales, gradually increasing your readership and managing your cash flow well enough for each issue of the magazine to pay for the next one. But if and when you get to the stage where you're showing a profit, it will be time to make some decisions. Perhaps you'll invest everything straight back into creating content. Do you want to expand – use the funds to increase your print run, send out a batch of promotional copies to potential advertisers, hold events to promote the magazine and generate new revenue streams, even invest in office space or better equipment for the space you have? Or do you want to keep some of that profit and finally take a holiday, or pay yourself a bit for the Herculean time and effort you've invested?

If you've survived the first year or two and managed to make the magazine pay for itself, you're already doing brilliantly. The title has a good reputation, your content is getting attention and the design has hit its stride. People in your industry and your target readership are taking an interest and buying your mag. You have something with weight, but the question now is how to turn that hard work and the respect you've earned into a sustainable financial future.

> "The reputation of the magazine is really good and content gets better each issue. So we have something of weight, but the question is, how do we do something with it that is really sustainable?"
>
> Erin Spens, *Boat*

Keep developing your editorial

You've inspired some imitators, so keep ahead of the field. If you are in the independent sector, chances are you have your niche, and that means limited market share. You must stay one step ahead of the titles snapping at your readership and advertisers.

Consistently producing brilliant editorial – and sometimes surprising your readers as well as making sure you live up to their expectations – is a good place to start. 'We are determined to continue to improve the quality of our journalism, photography and design,' says Matthew Lee of *Delayed Gratification*. 'Since our launch, as the world's first "slow journalism" magazine, several other print and online publications have joined the movement. We want to ensure we remain at the forefront ... by focusing on in-depth, long-form stories that help enhance our readers' understanding of the lasting impact of news events.'

If you keep the faith and stay true to the vision on which you built your early success, you will gain the confidence to evolve in your own way. 'You have to do three issues of a magazine to really know what you are doing,' reflects Veronica Ditting, art director of *The Gentlewoman*. 'In issue 3 we found our tone of voice visually, we changed paper stock and we were less rigid on our design than the first couple of issues … By issue 3 we all felt a bit more confident in what we were doing.'

Increase your distribution

If you started with a DIY distribution model, slow but steady growth over the first couple of years might get you to the position where volume of sales makes that physically impossible. It's time to get a professional distribution deal.

If you have already used a mix of direct sales and professional distribution, you should reach a point where you need to diversify your distribution. You may have a feel for untapped markets where it looks likely that you can tap into a bigger readership (analysing your online readership is a great indicator of this). 'We're going to start printing and distributing in North America, to fix the retail cost there,' says Rosa Park of *Cereal*. 'I believe we can dramatically increase our presence there, but only if we manage the selling cost, which is very difficult at the moment because of how much it costs to ship the magazine to the States from the UK.'

Titles that started out with smaller distributors catering to the independent market may grow to a point where they can explore more commercial options. *Cereal*'s admirable growth – from 1,500 to 25,000 copies in the first two years – meant that it was able to enjoy beneficial distribution deals in more commercial markets, and is now stocked in the first-class lounges of several airlines at airports around the world, as well as in shops and news-stands.

In 2014 Park also recognized that it would be a good moment to work with WHSmith Travel, supplying airports and railway stations. 'Entering WHSmith was something I wanted to do last, because it is a very mass-market, "high-street" place to be,' she says. 'I think as an independent title, your strength is not your numbers but your brand positioning and what kind of people you're targeting. So you cannot dilute that. I think growing is good, but growing too fast is bad. For us, we were adamant to grow at a pace we were comfortable with, where we weren't alienating certain stockists and readers, but at the same time reaching a bigger audience over time.'

"You have to grow constantly … Everything is so fast-paced, everything is non-stop – you can't just sit there – you have to be looking at what you're doing next to keep your readers interested."

Rosa Park, *Cereal*

Never not working: invent to survive

Makeshift

Frequency: Quarterly
Date launched: September 2011
Location: Virtual
Print run: 4,000
Cover price: $15

The people behind *Makeshift* know that innovation is crucial to survival. 'We're continuing to grow our readership and experiment with new revenue streams,' says *Makeshift*'s founding director, Steve Daniels. 'We've adopted a lot of practices from the growth-hacking movement – generating new leads and optimizing the sales funnel on our website. We're most excited about a series of design research workshops we're about to launch under a programme called the Makeshift Institute.' The magazine uses an innovative staff networking model and offers subscriptions incentives as rewards for sharing on social media. As the magazine puts it: 'Ingenuity is everywhere.'

Cereal

Frequency: Quarterly
Date launched: December 2012
Location: Bath
Print run: 25,000
Cover price: £10

Cereal is a great example of a magazine and an editorial team that never stands still. The clear and distinctive voice and visual style of its creators, Rosa Park and Rich Stapleton, is applied not only to the magazine but also to revenue-generating offshoots ranging from a service designing advertisements to product collaborations, pop-up shops, workshops and travel guides. At the time of writing they were also working on a new literary title and a permanent shop in *Cereal*'s home town, Bath. Park is extremely proactive about the magazine's distribution, which accounts for its phenomenal growth – from 1,500 copies to 25,000 copies in the two years since its launch.

Diversify

Once your magazine has hit its stride, you can start to indulge the ideas part of your brain and broaden your business. Events, new products and publications that complement what you already do can add to your revenue streams and help you towards sustainability and profit.

You might also expand your editorial in different directions by offering services as a creative agency, or set up a shop or other sideline. The key is to stay true to what you're good at and know what your readership and therefore your market will go for. *Wrap* magazine is a great example: this illustration magazine built up credibility and a great roster of contributors in its early years, then translated these into a shop, selling its own products and those of the makers and illustrators who contributed to the magazine.

For some indie magazines, diversifying is not just about growing but about survival, too. Will Hudson of INT Works and *Printed Pages* explains how he has taken a modular approach to building new aspects of his business. 'Increasingly, I don't think *Printed Pages* would exist if we were just a magazine,' he says. 'Nowadays, you need to have a number of things that go on. It comes back to the idea that if you're a big publisher you can have poorly performing issues every now and again and it kind of balances itself out, but for independents that can be crippling. We have the luxury that, with the online side and the sales that brings in, with the events and some of the special projects that we do, there isn't that pressure on the magazine to be hugely profitable to contribute to that stuff.'

1.

2.

Take stock

After a year of publishing you will be in a position to step back from the mayhem of launching and take stock of your performance. As well as considering adding more to your output as a magazine or as a brand, it might also be a time to streamline: to take a long hard look at what is working and what is not working. You might have to be brutal with yourself and make difficult changes.

'I had become engulfed in the creative process,' Cathy Olmedillas recalls of the first five years publishing *Anorak*. 'I thought "It breaks even, and does fine" – I never really worried about it. But two years ago I tried to turn it from a project into a proper full-time enterprise. The challenge then was to forget a bit about the creative and get the commercial side going. I chased shops and brands and got advertisers on board, took on an advertising salesperson … I had to stop having a studio and find the most cost-effective printers. Sometimes it meant severing relationships that had been going for four or five years. It's been so bloody hard, but ultimately it's been great.'

3.

Celebrate your landmarks

Just surviving can be a major achievement in the independent publishing world, so pat yourself on the back and reward your achievements. These could be apparently small but significant steps like finally getting into that elusive dream retailer, or hiring someone to clean the office toilets rather than doing it yourself. 'We just had "Port Publishing" engraved in steel on the building,' says Kuchar Swara of *Port*. 'There's a certain permanence about it. It's the same feeling as when we bought barcodes for four issues ahead: it means you think you're going to be in business for at least a year. At the time, we had no indication we'd be in business a week later, let alone four issues.'

4.

1. *Wrap* has an online shop selling products by the illustrators featured in the magazine, including its famous gift wrap collections

2. *Cereal's* online shop includes specially made products created in collaboration with carefully chosen brands

3. *Anorak* magazine subscription promotion

4. *Anorak* magazine holiday bundle with activity book

Reference
Little black book/
Glossary/Index

Indie-friendly retailers,
distributors, printers,
events, societies,
awards, websites,
books and reference
tools

Little black book

Here is a selection of handy resources to help you find the partners to build your publishing model and the events and societies that will help you play a role in the independent publishing world. It is by no means exhaustive but should give you a launch pad to help make your plans and ideas a reality.

Distributors

Distribution companies used by the independent magazines featured in this book.

Global
Central Books
London, UK

COMAG Specialist
London, UK

Dawson Media
UK (distribution to airlines and rail operators)

Export Press
Paris, France

Worldwide Magazine Distribution
Birmingham UK

UK and Europe
Antenne
London, UK

EM News
Belfast and Dublin

MMS
London, UK

Motto
Berlin, Germany

Revolver Publisher
Germany

RA & Olly
London, UK

North America
New Distribution House
New York, US and Montreal, Canada

Ubiquity
New York, US

Australasia
Mag Nation
Melbourne, Australia and Auckland, New Zealand

Perimeter
Melbourne, Australia

Online
Bruil & van de Staaij
bruil.info

Magpile
magpile.com

Magazine Shack
magazine-shack.co.uk

Newsstand
newsstand.co.uk

Independent retailers

A selection of international retailers stocking independent magazines.

UK and Europe
Artwords
artwords.co.uk

Athenaeum Boekhandel
athenaeum.nl

Banner Repeater
bannerrepeater.org

Castor & Pollux
store.castorandpollux.co.uk

Coffee Table Mags
coffeetablemags.myshopify.com

Colours May Vary
colours-may-vary.com

Correspondances
correspondances-shop.ch

do you read me?!
doyoureadme.de

Donlon Books
donlonbooks.com

Foyles
foyles.co.uk

Gudberg Nerger
gudbergnerger.com

Hordaland Kunstsenter
kunstsenter.no

Ideas On Paper
ideasonpapernottingham.co.uk

International Magazine Store
imstijdschriften.be

KK Outlet
kkoutlet.com

Koenig Books
buchhandlung-walther-koenig.de

Kunstgriff
kunstgriff.ch

Lorem (not ipsum)
loremnotipsum.com

Loring Art
loring-art.com

Magasand
magasand.com

Magazine Brighton
magazinebrighton.com

Magma
magmabooks.com

Material
materialmaterial.com

Motta
mottakunstboeken.nl

Mzin
mzin.de

No Guts No Glory
ngngdesign.com

Nook
nooklondon.com

Ofr Shop
ofrsystem.com

Page Five
pagefive.com

Papercut
papercutshop.se

Papersmith's
papersmiths.co.uk

pro qm
pro-qm.de

Provide
provideshop.com

Sérendipité
serendipite.ch

Soda
sodabooks.com

Soma
soma.gallery

Super Salon
supersalon.org

The Library Project
photoireland.org

Thisispaper
thisispaper.com

Village Bookstore
villagebookstore.co.uk

West Berlin
westberlin-bar-shop.de

X Marks the Bokship
bokship.org

<u>North America</u>
McNally Jackson
mcnallyjackson.com

Objectify
objectify139.com

Quimby's
quimbys.com

Soop Soop
soopsoop.ca

Spoonbill & Sugartown
spoonbillbooks.com

<u>Asia</u>
Basheer Graphic Books
basheergraphic.wordpress.com

Books Actually
booksactuallyshop.com

The Magazine Shop
themagazineshop.tumblr.com

Magpie
magpie.com.sg

Paper Cup
papercupstore.com

The U Cafe
www.underscoremagazine.com

The Yard
theyard-kw.com

<u>Australasia</u>
Beautiful Pages
beautifulpages.com.au

Künstler
kunstler.com.au

Mag Nation
magnation.com

Perimeter Books
perimeterbooks.com

World Food Books
worldfoodbooks.com

Events

C'mon to Papel, Spain
comeontopapel.com

Indie Con, Germany
wasistindie.de
indiemags.de

Facing Pages biennale,
the Netherlands
facingpages.org

MagFest, UK
magfest.co.uk

Modern Magazine conference, UK
magculture.com

Print Out, UK
magculture.com

Societies

British Society of Magazine Editors (BSME)
bsme.com

Editorial Design Organisation (EDO)
editorialdesign.org

Little Magazine Coalition (LMC)
thelittlemagazinecoalition.com

Professional Publishers Association (PPA)
ppa.co.uk

The Society of Publication Designers (SPD)
spd.org

Awards

BSME Awards

Magpile Awards

Society of Publication Designers Competition

Websites

Athanaeum Blog
athenaeumnieuwscentrum.
blogspot.co.uk

Coverjunkie
coverjunkie.com

Linefeed
linefeed.me

The Magazine Diaries
magazinediaries.com

MagCulture
magculture.com/blog

Stack
stackmagazines.com

The Stack on Monocle 24
monocle.com/radio/shows/the-stack

Books

Ruth Jamieson, *Print is Dead. Long Live Print* (Prestel, 2014)

Robert Klanten and A. Mollard, *Behind the Zines* (Gestalten Verlag, 2011)

Andrew Losowsky, *Fully Booked* (Gestalten, 2013)

Andrew Losowsky, *We Love Magazines* (Gestalten, 2007)

Andrew Losowski, *We Make Magazines* (Gestalten, 2009)

Jeremy Leslie, *The Modern Magazine* (Laurence King, 2013)

Teal Triggs, *Fanzines* (Thames & Hudson, 2010)

Glossary

This list does not provide an exhaustive guide to all printing, typographic and publishing terms but offers a guide to some of the unfamiliar terminology that you may encounter as someone new to independent magazine publishing.

'A' sizes
Metric paper sizes, e.g. A0, A1, A2 and so on.

ABC
A commercial magazine may refer to itself as being 'ABCed', meaning that its circulation has been audited by the Audit Bureau of Circulation. This industry standardized method of officially tracking circulation figures is traditionally used as a sales tool in advertising sales but is less important and rarely employed by independent magazines.

Advertorial
Advertising that mimics the tone and style of editorial but is paid for by an advertiser. Generally written and designed by the magazine's team, it must be sign-posted, e.g. 'advertorial' or 'sponsored content'.

Barcode
Code made up of numbers and parallel lines that is machine readable and which indicates certain information about a product.

Baseline
A typographic term indicating the line on which a row of letters sits.

Bleed
The edge of an image or layout that extends beyond the area to be trimmed. A bleed is included on images and layouts to account for the fact that slight slippage can occur in the printing and trimming process, and to ensure that this does not result in unwanted edges appearing. Printers usually require a 3 mm bleed.

Body copy
The main text of an article.

Bound-in insert
A section of pages bound in to the main part of the magazine that is outside of the main pagination and can be a different size and on a different paper stock.

Bound-in section
A section of pages (in a signature) that is on a different stock but bound in to the main part of the magazine. Bound-in sections must fall between signatures in the main magazine.

Box-out
A short pice of text additional to the main article, often placed in a box or separate area in the layout.

Classified
Advertisments in a text format, typically as a list or small cells at the back of the magazine.

CMYK
Cyan, Magenta, Yellow, Key (black): the four 'process' colours that can be used to print all colour images.

Coated paper
Paper that has been coated and gives a smooth shiny surface, commonly used for magazines.

Contra deal
A commercial exchange, for example with an advertiser or sponsor, where goods or services change hands instead of money.

Contract publishing
Magazines made as a promotional vehicle for a company or brand. The classic example is an airline's in-flight magazine.

Contributing editor
An editor who is not on the in-house staff of a magazine but who contributes ideas, articles and is consulted on the editorial direction of the title.

Copy-editor/sub-editor
The person responsible for checking text and layouts for errors and inconsistencies.

Cover mount
A 'giveaway', e.g. a booklet, affixed to the front of the magazine and often bagged along with it.

CPM
Term relating to online advertising; cost per mille, or cost of advertising per 1,000 clicks.

Display ad
Advertising, usually with visuals, where the artwork is supplied by the client; as opposed to text-only classified ads.

Distributor
An agent between publishers and retailers, handling management and delivery.

DPS
A double-page spread.

Dummy
A blank physical copy of a publication, produced by a printer to give an idea of size, binding style, paper stock and so on.

Editor's letter
The editor's introduction to each issue, typically one page, discussing prevailing interests and drawing attention to certain features of the issue.

Editorial meeting
Where the ideas for each issue are born and discussed, assignments allocated, plans are laid and general editorial direction reviewed. Ideally conducted in the pub.

Extent
The total number of pages in the publication.

Fair use
A term referring to the (rare) occasions when you are allowed to use images for free, in such a way that you are not directly profiting from their use, usually for creative or reportage purposes.

Fanzine
A cult or unofficial publication made by amateur enthusiasts.

FH
Front half of the magazine.

Flat plan
A list, table or diagram mapping out the entire page run of a magazine; used to plan the position of editoral and advertising pages, and to indicate production features such as stock changes.

Folio
The page number.

Footer
Any text appearing at the bottom of page layouts, e.g. title, page number, extra information.

Format
The size, shape and binding style of your magazine.

Four-colour process
Or CMYK: the 'process' colours used in printing.

Frequency
How often your magazine is published, most often monthly, bi-monthly, quarterly, bi-annually or annually.

FSC certified
Paper stock certified by the Forest Stewardship Council as being from sustainable sources. You can apply to FSC for authorization to use the logo on your masthead if the paper you use meets their criteria.

Fulfilment
The act of fulfilling an order, e.g. delivering your magazine to the customer.

Grid
The framework on which a designer lays out a magazine's pages.

GSM
Grams per square metre: the unit usually used to indicate paper density or thickness.

Gutter
The area at the centre of a double-page spread where the pages meet. It must be generous enough to allow for the area of paper concealed by the binding.

Hard proof
Proofs supplied on paper.

Header
The text elements that appear at the top of a page, e.g. section heads and titles.

House ad
An ad space used to promote an in-house message, e.g. subscriptions, special offers, events or products.

IBC
Inside back cover.

IFC
Inside front cover.

Imposition
A printing term: the non-sequential arrangement of a magazine's pages in an order that maximizes efficiency by getting the most number of trimmed pages out of a single sheet of paper.

ISSN
International Standard Serial Number: the essential code for any periodical that is to be sold at retail. Once you have received an ISSN you can buy barcodes.

Kerning
A typographic term indicating the spacing between letters.

Kill fee
A fee paid to a writer, photographer or illustrator for work commissioned but not published.

Leading
A typographic term indicating the spacing between lines of text.

Loose insert
A printed card or leaflet loosely inserted into the magazine. Can be sold to advertisers or used to promote the interests of the magazine, e.g. a subscription form or flyer promoting special offers, events or products.

Masthead
Used to describe the title of the magazine on the cover, but also the page in the magazine where staff and key information such as contacts and publishing information are listed.

Media pack or kit
A document, which can be digital or printed, that sums up your magazine and its commercial offering.

OBC
Outside back cover.

Offset litho
Offset lithography: the most common form of non-digital printing for publications, whereby images, text and layouts are re-created on a metal plate, which is then transferred on to rubber rollers and eventually on to paper.

Overhead
The costs of running your business that are not directly related to the product, e.g. office rent and utilities.

Pagination
Defining the page sequence of the magazine, including the cover. For example, a magazine with 96 inner pages and an ordinary cover is expressed as 96 + 4.

Perfect binding
A binding method where pages are glued together, giving the publication a square-edged spine.

PMS
The Pantone matching system for specifying print colours.

Point size
A typographic term indicating the size of letters used in a text layout.

Pre-press
A printing term referring to the preparation of magazine files between the layout process and actual printing, e.g. adjusting images and creating printing plates.

Press check
A final round of proofing after the print set-up is ready but before actual printing begins.

Print run
The number of copies of a publication to be printed. You will specify a print run to your printer.

Process colours
Cyan, Magenta, Yellow, Key (black), or CMYK: the four colours used in the printing process.

Proofreading
The process of checking the text and layouts of a magazine for errors and inconsistencies.

Proofs
Digital or printed versions of your finished magazine, used for proofreading and final checking of artwork before going to print. The first round of proofs for your proofreader can be run out on a standard office printer. Once any editorial amends have be made, the layout finalized and artwork sent to your printer, s/he will then supply a final set of proofs to be checked by editorial and design staff. At this stage you're looking to ensure the 'big things' are correct – pages in the right place, colours looking good and so on.

Publishing schedule
Your schedule for key points in the publishing cycle, including copy deadline; artwork and production deadline; when you will have copies back from the printer; and on-sale date.

Pull quote
A quote extracted from an article and enlarged in the layout, used to pique reader interest and draw them through the article.

PUR binding
A method of biding that is often chosen over perfect binding, generally because its use of polyurethane reactive adhesive is thought to be stronger, allowing a magazine to lay flat when open without breaking the binding.

Rate card
The full price listed for an advertisement in the media pack – usually a jumping-off point for negotiations.

ROP/run of print
An advertising term, referring to an advert that can be placed at any point in the main section of the magazine, as opposed to an ad that is bought to go in a specific page position.

Run-on/overrun
Copies printed extra to the specified print run.

Signature
Pages collated in the right order for printing on a sheet, so that when they are trimmed and bound the spreads fall correctly. Typically signatures are 16 pages, but they can also be 8 or 4.

Soft proof
Digitally supplied proofs.

Spot colour
A colour printed using its own separation plate, outside of the four plates used for the standard process colours of cyan, magenta, yellow and black.

Spot varnish
An area of varnish overprinted on a particular area, often used to pick out elements on a cover, for example the magazine's title.

Spread
Two pages opposite each other.

Stet
Proofreaders' term meaning 'let it stand' – used if a change has been marked up by the proofreader but they want to reverse it.

Stock
The type of paper you will print on. Often magazines will use different weight or styles of stock for different elements, e.g. the cover.

Style guide
Set of rules for a title's set conventions of language and typography — for example, the way numbers are written or whether job titles are capitalized.

Subs
Subscriptions.

Subs swap
When two publications exchange subscriptions free of charge.

Substrate
A material used for printing, e.g. paper or cardboard.

Syndication
Part of the content created for a magazine, e.g. a feature article that is sold on for use in other titles.

Tip-in
An extra printed element, e.g. an image or postcard attached (usually with a dab of glue) to the surface of a page in the magazine.

Trim marks
Lines printed at the corners of a magazine's pages to indicate where the paper should be cut to get the final page size.

Two-colour process
Printing using only two colours (these can be process colours or spot colours).

Uncoated paper
An alternative to coated paper, more textured and less glossy in appearance, that has been widely adopted by independent magazines, often as a point of difference to the look and feel of commercially published magazines.

Uniques
Term relating to website analytics; the number of 'unique impressions' or visits to a page by an individual, usually measured over the space of a month.

Voucher copy
A free copy of the magazine sent to advertisers or PRs as a promotional tool.

Index

Page numbers in **bold** refer to illustrations

Image credits

All images are courtesy of and © of the magazine unless otherwise stated below or in the caption.
T = top; B = bottom; L = left; R = right; C = centre

7TR Design: Willem Stratmann/ Studio Anti **7CL** Creative Director: David Lane **7BR** The Slow Journalism Company **8TL** Creative Director: Kuchar Swara **8TR** Own It! Publishing **9** Photo: Max Creasy **10TL** *The Gourmand*, Creative Director: David Lane **10TR** *Monocle* **10B** *It's Nice That* **11** Design: Kai von Tabenau **13T** Design Director: Dylan Fracareta © FEBU Publishing **14T** Creative Director: David Lane **15B** The Slow Journalism Company, cover art: Shepard Fairey **16–20 (all)** Courtesy Dazed Media **16** Photo © Brantley Gutierrez **18** Photo © Nick Knight **19** Photo © Rankin **20L+R** Photo © Collier Schorr **22TL** *Delayed Gratification*, The Slow Journalism Company, cover art: Eelus **22TR** *Port*, photo: Robin Broadbent **22B** *Wrap* **23** © Die Brueder–Malte Spindler **24B** Jean Jullien for Wrap **26T** Own It! Publishing **26B** Photo: Ilvio Gallo and Nathalie Du Pasquier **27T** © Acid and 19-80 Éditions **31T+B** The Slow Journalism Company **31T** Cover art: Eelus **38TL** Colin Caradec and Morgane Rébulard, *The Shelf* **38TR** Kai Brach, *Offscreen* © Mark Lobo **38B** Elana Schlenker, *Gratuitous Type*, photo: Ross Mantle **44T** Robin Broadbent, styled by Sam Logan **44CL** Backyard Bill **44CR** David Hughes **44B** Amber Rowlands, styled by Sam Logan **45 (all)** Editor: Rachel Taylor, Creative Director: Jody Daunton **45TL** cover artist Bryan Schutmaat **45TR** 'Korean Papermaking: Paper, People, Place'; subject in photo and author: Aimee Kee, photo: Ricky Rhodes **45B** cover artist Jack Latham **52TL** *LAW* **52TR** *Perdiz*, photo: Borja Ballbé and Querida Studio **54B** *Oh Comely* **54TL**

Centerfold featuring Letterproeftuin **54TR** Emmet Byrn, photo: Peter Happel Christian **54B** Cover photo: Jim Campers **55 (all)** Creative Direction: David Lane **58TL** Illustration: Pat Bradbury for Wrap **58CL** Illustrations: Jean Jullien **58CR** Illustration: Atelier Bingo for Wrap **58BR** Artwork: Martin Nicolausson for Wrap **59C** Illustration: Studio Tipi **61T** Image detail: Otis Shepard © *Eye* magazine **61B** Design Director: Dylan Fracareta © FEBU Publishing **62T** Brian Eno, Design: Kai von Tabenau, Portrait: Matt Anker **62B** Design: Ariane Spanier **65TL** Photo: Max Creasy **65TR** The Slow Journalism Company **66T+TCL** Design: Human After All **68CL** The Slow Journalism Company **69T** Illustration: Karen Klink, Art Director: Jade George, Creative Director: Rawan Gebran **71–75** © *Eye* magazine **76TL** *Makeshift* **76TR** Photo © June Kim **76B+77** Photo: Max Creasy **78T** The Slow Journalism Company **79T** Photo: Max Creasy **81T** Photo © June Kim **83T** Photo: Andy Kirkpatrick **83C** Photo: Lukasz Warzecha **83BL** Photo: Martin Hartley **83BR** Photo: Cat Vinton **88TL** *Works That Work* **88TR** Motto Books **88B+89** Antenne Books Ltd. **94 (all)** Art Director: Jessica Lowe **94TL** Photo: Takashi Homma **94TR** Photo: Gavin Green **94B** Illustrator: Olimpia Zagnoli **96** Antenne Books Ltd. **97T** Ryan Fitzgibbon at Stack Live © Helen Cathcart **97B** © Die Brueder–Malte Spindler **98TL** Interview: Kati Krause, portrait: Marlen Mueller **98TR** Illustration: Kate Copeland **98B** Illustration: Alexander Wells **99 (all)** published by A Small Press (Australia) and Ilam Press (New Zealand); edited, designed and

printed: Luke Wood and Stuart Geddes **99CL** words and images: Juan Metrez **99CR** words and images: Anna Dean **101+103 (all)** The Slow Journalism Company **103CL** Cover art: Ai Weiwei **103B** Cover art: Pablo Delgado **104** © Stack magazines Ltd. **105T** Photo: Beinta á Torkilsheyggi, model: Jessie Dunn, styling and background: Verity **107** Courtesy Marc Robbemond **108** Petra Noordkamp **110TL** *Disegno*, photo: Ola Bergengren, styling and set design: Iwa Herdensjö **110B** *Offscreen* **115T** Photo: Pieter Hugo, creative director: Kuchar Swara **115C** Photo: Stefan Heinrichs, styling: David St John James **115BL** Photo: Nadav Kander, creative directors: Matt Willey and Kuchar Swara **115BR**: Photo: Robin Broadbent **121B** Design: Human After All **128T** *Cereal* **128C** *Perdiz*, feature on Pixy Liao's photographs, photo: Borja Ballbé and Querida Studio **128B** *Port*, photo: Stefan Heinrichs, styling: David St John James **130T** Jake Beeby, photo: Elliot Kennedy **130B** Photo: Borja Ballbé and Querida Studio **133T** © Anja Aronowsky Cronberg, publisher **140TL** *Offscreen* © Kai Brach **140TR** © Die Brueder–Malte Spindler **140BR** Ryan Fitzgibbon at Stack Live © Helen Cathcart **141** © Kai Brach **143T** Olivia Williams photographed by Alasdair McLellan **143B** Photo: Sarah Keough **144** Handsome Frank Ltd., cover illustration: Tim McDonagh **145T+B** © Die Brueder–Malte Spindler **152TR** *Wrap* **152TL+B** *Cereal* **155T** Photo: Jeroen Toirkens **157T** Illustration: Amandine Urruty **158T** *Monocle* **158CL** Motto Books **158B** Offscreen, Photo © June Kim